WORK

WORK

The Building Of The Channel Tunnel Rail Link

Stephen Bayley

MERRELL
LONDON • NEW YORK

CONTENTS

FOREWORD

The construction of High Speed 1, on time and within budget, is a great British success story. It is a modern engineering feat that connects vision with enterprise, innovation with delivery and Victorian splendour with iconic design.

This is the country's first major railway project for over 100 years, firmly linking the UK into the rapidly expanding European high speed rail network, cutting journey times to continental Europe, and acting as a powerful catalyst for massive regeneration. This has always been, and always will be, far more than just a railway.

This is an historic moment that leaves a legacy of substantial benefits now and for future generations. I believe that in years to come we will look back at this project as being a highlight of the decade. I congratulate London & Continental Railways, the pioneering engineers, architects and everyone who has been involved. We should all be proud of this momentous achievement.

Gordon Brown

The Rt Hon. Gordon Brown MP, Prime Minister

PREFACE

When the rich man travels, or if he lies in bed all day, his capital remains undiminished and perhaps his income flows in all the same. But when a poor man travels he has not only to pay his fare but to sink his capital, for his time is his capital; and if he now consumes only five hours instead of ten in making a journey, he has saved five hours in time for useful labour – useful to himself, his family and to society. Sir James Allport, General Manager of the Midland Railway (builders of the original St Pancras station), 1880s

As a child, I never much cared for the romance of rail travel. On the contrary, I found stations and trains scary. Childhood visits to Liverpool's Lime Street station gave me lasting memories of fearful Satanic noise and dirt, of sad partings. At the time I did not realize that this cacophonous cavern of iron and glass was built by the London and North Western Railway in 1849 as a symbol of all that Victorian railways wanted to offer: personal freedom and corporate identity, a curious but benign cocktail of capitalism, technology, democracy and opportunity. That combination is about to have its day once again. A station such as Liverpool Lime Street was not only great engineering, but also great advertising. I knew none of this as I waved my grandmother goodbye with one hand while trying to keep the deafening sound out with the other. Liverpool's train shed was, until surpassed by that of Birmingham New Street five years later, the world's greatest single-span structure. Knowing none of this, I did not then imagine a future for rail.

The trains of my childhood were dark, hissing and threatening. The stations were grim necessities, not discretionary delights for the sophisticated traveller. In the intervening years things have changed. The age of the jet was in its infancy when I was a boy in Lime Street. But now its moment has come and gone: within a few years air travel rapidly deteriorated from being a privileged, romantic indulgence into a humiliating ordeal. And the car? Well, the indulgent daydreams – indeed, realities – of luxury mobility I enjoyed in the back seat of a Humber or an Austin Westminster or a Jaguar have evaporated, too. The car might remain as an important symbol in our daily trials of social competition and cultural modelling, but its viability as rational transport has been completely undermined by its popularity. The technological competence of the modern car is mocked by the non-negotiable congestion it causes. Factor in environmental anxieties, and it looks as though the time is five minutes to midnight for the automobile industry as we know it.

Now I have come to think of rail travel as one of civilization's pleasures, one that long ago surpassed the grim tribulations of air travel in its combination of comfort and convenience. And, increasingly, speed. Parts of this book were written at more than 300 kilometres per hour travelling through southern England and northern France, in a lightly pressurized and pleasantly air-conditioned environment. Fifty years ago Marshall McLuhan coined the expression 'electric speed' to describe how video media appeared to accelerate life. He had no idea that Eurostar and a laptop would make electric speed even more deliriously intoxicating. And an everyday reality for people who want to travel.

But there have been other changes, too. Since my early visits to Liverpool Lime Street, British attitudes to Europe have evolved. In 1930 the governmental Peacock Committee published a report about the desirability of a Channel Tunnel. One of its fears was that Britain would, after many thousands of years of isolation in its cold northern waters, again have a land frontier with the Continent, the first since prehistoric travellers ventured across the undifferentiated landmass of Europe when sabre-toothed tigers prowled and groups convened in caves to consider the future of the wheel. The Peacock Committee was concerned that any new Channel Tunnel, far from being a 'fixed link' to Europe and a longed-for liberation from insularity, might result in 'undesirable reactions of a social and moral kind'.

We are broader-minded today. To paraphrase, in fact to mangle, T.S. Eliot, we are not the same people who left the station, or the same ones who will arrive at the terminus while the narrowing rails slide together behind us. London has become a global cosmopolis and a new railway has made it closer to Paris, in terms both of time and of culture, than it is to Liverpool's Lime Street; it is now viable to have lunch in Paris and still be back in London by 6 pm. That's the wonder of high-speed rail. How civil engineering, optimism and vision made a dream come true is explained in the following chapters. It is not just a world of high-speed travel to lunch in Paris, but an alternative universe of asynchronous motors, catenaries, ultimate limit states, dead loads, skidding beams, push-jacks and intermediate deviators. Whizzing through the Nord-Pas-de-Calais, musing, perhaps, on Emile Zola's epic accounts of the tribulations of the Nord miners, or Van Gogh not far away, or the terrible ghost armies of the Somme, we have no need to think of these things. And, until I wrote that initial paragraph, I had all but forgotten about my childhood dread of trains and stations.

But the new generation of civilized traveller has good reason to be very glad that someone else has done all that hard work on the engineering: it is all but invisible, even though the benefits it brings are so tangible. The culture of rail travel is one thing, the technology another. But I am certain that at 300 kilometres per hour, it is as well to have your load paths secured by science.

Stephen Bayley
London, November 2007

INTROD

UCTION

'We do not ride the railroad; it rides upon us.'

Henry David Thoreau, 'Walden' (1854)

Why do we need high-speed rail? The question was answered by a Lancashire businessman active before Queen Victoria came to the throne in 1837:

> We must determine … whether it is desirable that a nation should continue in the quiet enjoyment of pastoral or agricultural life, or that it should be launched into the bustle and excitement of commerce and manufacture. It must be admitted that the golden age is past, and it is to be feared that the iron age has succeeded. The locomotive engine and railway were reserved for the present day. From west to east, and from north to south, the mechanical principle, the philosophy of the nineteenth century, will spread and extend itself. The world has received a new impulse. The genius of the age, like a mighty river of a new world, flows onward, full, rapid, and irresistible.
>
> Henry Booth, Treasurer of the Liverpool and Manchester Railway, 1830

This is the Age of the Train Version 2.0. Europe's high-speed train operators now offer the prospect of seamless rail travel to and from London; Britain is not quite the island it once was. Thirteen years to the day after the Channel Tunnel opened for business, a dedicated high-speed track between London and Paris became a reality. This track was always known among officials as the Channel Tunnel Rail Link (CTRL), but travellers are to call it High Speed 1 (HS1). The geography of Britain has changed. Horizons have broadened.

The first railway passengers found the unprecedented experience of train travel quite literally astonishing. In 1835 one Charles Young rode the Liverpool to Manchester railway, writing excitedly to his sister: 'It is impossible to form any idea of the rapidity of moving' (he was travelling at perhaps nearly 50 kilometres per hour, but up to that point no person – apart, that is, from someone who had fallen off a building – had ever travelled faster than a horse). But then the excitement of speed gave way to second thoughts about the aesthetics: 'I am much disappointed in the view of the country, the railway being cut through so many hills you have frequently for miles only clay mounds on each side of you – consequently no splendid prospect can attract your attention.' These new railways went through uncorrupted country, reaching into cities that did not yet have suburbs, and were not compromised by tarmac roads, electrical cabling, drains, tubes or any of the other obstructive infrastructure that powers and exhausts the modern city.

But this new railway is very different. It has been built not ruthlessly through unspoilt nineteenth-century Lancashire, but sensitively through one of the planet's greatest megalopolises during the very busy and crowded early years of the twenty-first century. It threads a path between London's massive,

Top King's Cross was built in 1850 on the site of an old smallpox and fever hospital, and opened to the public in 1852 after a period devoted to freight. Queen Victoria used the station to travel to the York races in 1853.

Above The pseudo-Modernist concourse was added to King's Cross in the 1970s, painfully compromising the original purity of the façade.

Opposite, top The extent of the blighted 'railway lands' behind the contrasting and proud façades of St Pancras and King's Cross is clear when seen from the air.

Opposite, bottom Disruption at St Pancras caused by a Luftwaffe attack in August 1942. There is now a better sort of European visitor.

dark underground infrastructure and some of the world's most expensive real estate above it, then on to the prosperous suburbs and valuable agricultural land beyond. If the scale of such a colossal undertaking is not generally understood, it is because great care has been taken to avoid disruption, and to follow, wherever possible, existing routes. About a quarter of the 100 kilometres of this new railway is underground. At the old Connaught Hotel in London the waiters could, according to tradition, change the tablecloth halfway through dinner without disturbing the diners. Magnified to a scale costing £5 billion, such a feat has been achieved with this new railway.

No one understood the allure of the railway better than the writer Marcel Proust. He enjoyed the voyeuristic pleasures of guidebooks much more than he enjoyed books on art. But 'the motive force' of his 'exaltation' was the railway timetable. Here was 'the most intoxicating romance in the lover's library', the tabulated data on which dreams were based. For Proust, an element of the excitement of any railway journey involves sex. From the timetable he 'learned the ways of joining her there in the afternoon, in the evening, that very morning'.

Around-the-clock services promise us all a Proustian moment, with or without a tisane and a madeleine. But there are other wonders, too. HS1 is the first new mainline railway in Britain for about a hundred years. It is as simple, strange and shocking as that. The country that invented rail travel has, until now, had difficulty keeping up to date with its own darling, which, like so many other British innovations, has prospered better abroad.

To realize the extent of the achievement, it is useful to study an aerial photograph of the so-called King's Cross Railway Lands, north London, in about 1980 (opposite). The picture shows a scene of desperate neglect, desolation and desuetude. A terrible waste of spirit in an expense of shame: all those Victorian dreams mired in toxicity. Architects speak contemptuously of SLOAP, or 'Space Left Over After Planning'. The SLOAP of the King's Cross Railway Lands was filled with depressing mess. The once-proud King's Cross station was defaced by an execrable pseudo-Modernist extension built by British Rail in the 1970s. Intended as a temporary structure, it was never replaced as people cared so little. So it stood as insult and reprimand to ambition and progress. The once-glorious St Pancras station was filthy, its hotel long since deserted and turned into the drabbest of offices. Just imagine strip lighting, stained carpet tiles, peeling institutional paint, and the smell of rot and flatulent bureaucracy to get the effect. Behind the hotel, W.H. Barlow's great iron station roof – which easily humbled that of Lime Street – was rusting and encrusted in urban guano. Some of the glass had been damaged by Luftwaffe raids in the Second World War. Forty years after the last Heinkel dropped its deadly load on London N1, no one had got round to reglazing. The railways that had once been the pride of Britain were now a national disgrace.

HS1 is something of which even the sternest of Victorians might have been proud. It represents a more positive, more modern, better organized, more competent, more outgoing, more connected Britain. True, HS1 has been a long time coming. Britain might have been slow in starting high-speed rail travel – nearly thirty years behind the French, in fact – but those years were not wasted. The theory and practice of high-speed rail are now understood much better in Britain than they were in 1980. The huge success of the TGV has shown that it is not just a typically French *grand projet*, but a viable competitor to intra-European air travel.

The secret of really effective high-speed travel is immediate access to city centres. Brilliant and exemplary as the French TGV may be, its stations are often outside them. The financial and technological rationale of the TGV depended on dead-straight track usually passing through virgin land, so out-of-town stations were inevitable. At Avignon, for example, it is a ten-minute drive from the station

to the Rue Rempart Saint-Lazare in the city centre. But St Pancras is in central London, in an area that it is helping to revitalize. And HS1 has a station in the heart of Stratford, east London, now a centre of regeneration and one of the reasons for London's success in the bid for the 2012 Olympics.

A new railway is always an unusual and exciting thing: such is the expense and difficulty of building one, it is not something that happens very often (in Britain, it seems, about once every hundred years). Few governments, let alone private organizations, have the nerve and resources to do it. After some humiliating bungling with its own *grands projets*, Britain has managed to complete one successfully, although not without some tribulation. Throughout the building of HS1, and perhaps somewhat unusually, there was always a clarity of vision shared among the managers and the engineers. Completing the

project was a matter of confronting some difficult finances, entrenched cultures, demanding geology and technological challenges, not to mention the sometimes testing political realities of the county of Kent, the 'Garden of England'. There is no better description of this historic south-eastern county than that of Camden's *Britannia*. The following passage is from Richard Gough's translation of 1789. While the French were having a revolution, the British were considering their past:

> *The country at present called Kent is much diversified, being more level and woody to the west, and to the east rising with gentle hills. The inhabitants divide the south part along the Thames into three parts, or, as they call them, degrees, of which the uppermost on the Thames they account most healthy and rich; the lowermost rich, but unhealthy, being for the most part marshy, but producing most luxurious herbage. Almost the whole county abounds with meadows, pastures, and cornfields, is wonderfully fruitful in apples, as also cherries … It has many cities and towns, tolerably safe harbours, and some iron mines, but the air is somewhat thick from the vapours rising from the waters. The inhabitants still deserve that reputation for humanity which Caesar formerly gave them: not to mention their courage.*

This is one part of HS1: an audacious plan to drive a new railway through one of the most historic, beautiful and prosperous parts of Britain. This involved the construction of tunnels through the North Downs and a daredevil crossing of the River Medway. The other part was to burrow the new railway in demanding conditions underneath the River Thames and then to launch it into an amazing tunnel beneath east London to emerge suddenly in the greatest railway station in the world: St Pancras International. Once an advertisement for Victorian grandiosity, the station has been restored and translated with breathtaking skill and thoroughness into an advertisement for another vision, now a reality: reliable, effective, international high-speed rail travel.

Never mind the mountains of paper consumed and the cosmic infinities of hot air expended in the process, building HS1 involved excavating about

15 million cubic metres of soil from London and Kent. One of the significant novelties of the project has been the unusual amount of recycling. There has been very little waste. Brownfields have become green. In north Kent, spoil from the North Downs Tunnel was used in the Nashenden Valley, near Borstal, to form an embankment for the widening of the M2 motorway. Two million cubic metres of spoil from the London Tunnels and the Stratford Box were used to raise the site for Stratford City and the Olympic Athletes' Village by 7 metres. Water drained from the excavations in east London was sold to Thames Water and drunk by Londoners.

HS1 also involved the planting of 1,200,000 trees and the creation of 230 hectares of new woodland, 370 hectares of new grassland and 80 hectares of wildflower meadow, including the fine 'Eurostar Meadow' over a cut-and-cover tunnel at Mersham. This last was typical of the care taken to protect the environment during the construction of HS1. The old village of Mersham was unhelpfully bisected by the nineteenth-century London to Folkestone railway. The new high-speed line threatened even greater levels of disruption and inconvenience, and noise levels at the school that lies near the track would have been intolerable. Instead of relocating the school, it was decided to build new cut-and-cover tunnels over both the old and the new railways. As well as reducing existing and future noise levels, the Eurostar Meadow had the happy effect of reuniting the two halves of the village. A plaque dated 9 June 2003 now stands there to commemorate the end of civil-engineering works on Section 1. In addition, over the extent of the project 40 kilometres of hedgerow were planted, and seven new ponds and two new wetlands formed. Various dormouse colonies were relocated and a bat hibernaculum was established.

This new railway has some claim to be Europe's most ambitious construction project of recent years, and its primary purpose is to connect with that of the recent past: the Channel Tunnel. From 14 November 2007 travellers have been offered the final realization of what has been a dream since the first years of the railways: uninterrupted, fast travel to Europe on dedicated modern tracks.

Sir John Hawkshaw, engineer of the Severn Tunnel, proposed a Channel Tunnel between Dover and Calais in 1877.

The Channel Tunnel

To understand the importance of HS1, it is first necessary to understand the background to the building of the Channel Tunnel itself, and what underwater tunnels and tunnelling mean to an island nation such as Britain. Ten thousand years ago the River Thames was a tributary of the Rhine, and, if the cities had then existed, it would have been possible to walk overland from London to Rome. Now, the Channel Tunnel has blurred borders that have existed since before recorded history. It has become a vital artery, but was once seen as a threat to the security of Britain. Getting it built required not only physical bravery and audacious engineering, but also a redrawing of Britain's emotional frontiers.

The Channel itself is as much a psychological as a physical barrier, and has a meaning sedimented deep in cultural memory. Because the British sense of identity is historically dependent on it, the Channel has always been more British than French. With the liberation of borders by the Channel Tunnel and the very first Eurostars in 1994 came a sense of euphoria, blunted only by small hints of muddle. You can see this today at Ashford International station. A confused conception of Continental sophistication mingled with jingoism is revealed by the French drinks, German confectionery and Union Jacks at a facility known, in the Italian style, as the Gran Caffe. Still, the Tunnel brought Ashford and Calais closer together.

The idea of a tunnel under the Channel was first advanced in 1751 by the Amiens Academy, which announced a competition for the design of a new means of making the crossing. But the first realistic (if that is the right word) proposal was made to Napoleon Bonaparte in 1802 by a French mining engineer, Albert Mathieu. The plan, apparently made without any reference to the geological realities of the seabed, nor, indeed, to engineering possibilities,

Right Early Channel Tunnel proposals – this is by Hector Horeau – were often fantastic and unrealistic.

Below An impression of the Dover entrance to the Channel Tunnel, from 1858.

Bottom Visionaries were drawn to the challenge of submarine trains: pioneering film director Georges Méliès made *Tunnelling the English Channel* in 1907.

Pages 34–35 One of the two laser-guided Channel Tunnel TBMs.

involved turning the mid-Channel Varne Bank into an artificial island, from where one tunnel would go to France, another to Britain. We owe the true science of intercontinental submarine tunnelling to another Frenchman, Thomé de Gamond (1807–1875). He studied the Channel's seabed strata at first hand, at one stage descending 30 metres on a rope, using a 72-kilogram bag of pebbles as ballast, and without any breathing apparatus. Fortunately, and unexpectedly, he survived this appalling ordeal. He presented his designs to Queen Victoria, Prince Albert and Napoléon III, Emperor of France, in 1856 and received vocal support from Isambard Kingdom Brunel and Robert Stephenson. His plans were revised and presented again at the Exposition Universelle in Paris in 1867.

Of course, these plans were never realized, but concepts for a cross-Channel link continued to preoccupy inventive minds. In the mid-nineteenth century Hector Horeau, a French engineer living in London, proposed a tubular iron tunnel lying on the Channel seabed, exposed to the fish. He was sketchy about matters of insulation and waterproofing. In 1876 W.H. Barlow, the engineer of St Pancras station, published a paper on his proposal for crossing the Channel. It was reported in contemporary newspapers:

> *Mr W.H. Barlow proposed a submerged bridge, which was of steel tubes carried on piers. The idea has since been further worked out by [his son] Mr P.W. Barlow. The plan proposed is to make the tunnel of elastic iron or steel plates, riveted together, surrounded by brickwork laid in asphalt, and timber planking, secured by rings of copper. This tube may be constructed at shipbuilders' yards, in lengths of about three hundred feet, and towed to the proposed line of the railway using a floating iron coffer-dam.*

In 1889 engineers Schneider & Hersent proposed a bridge from Cap Gris Nez to a point near Folkestone, Kent. One million tons of steel, requiring repainting every four years, were to rest on masonry supports. An equally unrealistic competing scheme suggested an underwater barrage to carry a steam-powered transporter vehicle holding four trains above the roiling surface of the Channel.

These fabulous eccentricities made a conventional bored tunnel seem a blindingly obvious practical solution. While French visionaries dabbled with fanciful cross-Channel schemes, the British attended to more practical tunnelling matters. Warming Anglo-French relations after the Franco-Prussian War of 1870 led to the formation in 1872 of the English Channel Tunnel Company. Trial borings began at the bottom of Shakespeare Cliff in 1881, using early versions of what would become known as a tunnel-boring machine (TBM), manufactured by Beaumont & English and running on compressed air. But in the year of the

trial excavations a deteriorating political climate and military opposition to what was seen as a fast track for French invaders forced a halt. The continuation of Anglo-French cooperation seemed unlikely.

The tunnel scheme was revived in 1906 by a new Channel Tunnel Company working with l'Association du Chemin de Fer Sous-Marin entre la France et l'Angleterre. The aim now was to run twin tunnels carrying electric trains, but the First World War intervened. There were more trial borings in the 1920s, but in 1930 a timorous Imperial Defence Committee, known as the Peacock Committee, declared against providing that same entry point for invaders. Only in 1956 was the idea revived by a Study Group, and in 1963 a government White Paper finally gave official support. In 1973, after Britain's entry into the European Community, there was a final Anglo-French agreement, but, desperate to make economies after the oil crisis, the Labour government cancelled the project in 1975.

Britain under the premiership of Margaret Thatcher had a different mood. In 1981 British Rail, then a nationalized concern, agreed with the French railway operator SNCF to work on a tunnel. By 1985, in time for the deadline for the project, five proposals had been received. Euroroute, weirdly reminiscent of nineteenth-century engineering fantasies, was a submerged rail tunnel with islands and a bridge. Europont was a suspension bridge combined with a rail tunnel. Transmanche Express proposed parallel twin rail and twin road tunnels, while the Van der Putten proposal involved a dyke and a tunnel. The Trans-Manche/Channel Tunnel Group proposed the twin rail and single service tunnels that won the contract. The result was announced at Lille's Hotel de Ville on 20 January 1986. It was a striking moment of Anglo-French cooperation. On 29 July 1987 Mrs Thatcher and François Mitterrand, President of France, signed the Treaty of Canterbury, and the Channel Tunnel Act of 1987 gave the operating concession to Trans-Manche Link, a carefully negotiated bit of 'Franglais' nomenclature. Later, it was renamed EuroTunnel. The main contractors were a mixture of French and British companies, and during the process of boring Mrs Thatcher's pride was somewhat restored by British engineers being generally regarded as making better progress than their French counterparts. On 1 December 1990 Tunnel workers Philippe Cozette and Graham Fagg exchanged French and British flags underwater. The civil engineers had realized perhaps the most astonishing exercise in infrastructure of all time.

The Channel Tunnel opened to Eurostar services in 1994. In the same year Tony Blair succeeded the late John Smith as leader of the Labour Party in Britain, and George W. Bush was elected Governor of Texas. At the time, the Channel Tunnel might have represented old mechanics, not new-age technology, but it changed the way Britain looked at the world. Eight million cubic metres of spoil had been removed to create the tunnels, which can take thirty trains per hour. At any one time several thousand people are underwater. Many of them have anxieties about being in so unnatural a situation, but the geological reality is very reassuring: the strata underlying rivers and seas tend to be naturally waterproof, otherwise the water would simply drain away.

Congratulated on completing the Thames Tunnel in 1843, with its pioneering submarine tunnelling techniques (see pages 91–95), Marc Isambard Brunel wearily said, 'Néanmoins, si je l'avais à refaire je ferais mieux' ('Nevertheless, if I had to do it again, I would do better'). Maybe, but the Channel Tunnel needs little improvement. Tunnelling is conservative engineering: empiricism was long resistant to the advance of theory. The Channel Tunnel is the magnificent result of a European adventure that, according to myth, began when Virgil assembled 80,000 devils on a mountainside in Campania, Italy, and, overnight, they drove a passage through the rock, creating Europe's very first tunnel. It is almost as if Brunel had been invited to do it again, and had done it better.

A TRIP TO PARIS IN THE EIGHTEENTH CENTURY

The Englishman is only ever happy travelling south. There never was a Grand Tour to the north. As the great Samuel Johnson knew, 'a man who has not been in Italy is always conscious of an inferiority'. Johnson went on to explain that the 'object of travelling is to see the shores of the Mediterranean'. So it has always been the custom to head south for the English Channel.

In 1772 Dr Burney spent nine days waiting in Dover for a favourable wind to get him across the Channel. It was often a grisly journey, although Horatio Nelson, experienced in much worse hardships, did the trip in November 1783 in a 'fine north-west wind' and a brisk three-and-a-half hours. Mostly, arrivals in France were a mixture of exhaustion and gratitude. Percy Bysshe Shelley landed in 1814 'exhausted with sickness and fatigue', according to his *History of a Six Weeks' Tour* (1817). He walked across the sands and was immediately struck by the different buzz in the conversation and the fact that the men wore earrings. 'The manners', he said, 'are not English.' Lady Mary Wortley Montagu had noticed this in 1718: 'Staring is *à la mode* – there is a ... stare of curiosity, a stare of expectation, a stare of surprise,' always accompanied by a grin. Thomas Carlyle had difficulty finding any gentlemen on the streets of France.

Most tourists – then, as now – were in a hurry to get to Paris. Some might stop at Chantilly to see the gardens of the Prince Condé, or at Saint-Denis to admire the monuments to the French kings in the Abbey (where there was also a relic of the Virgin's hair, described by John Evelyn on his visit of 1643 as one of the Benedictines' 'authentic toys'). In the days of the Grand Tourists there were customs officials at Paris's *barrières*. When James Boswell was stopped by someone from the Bureau du Roi, his first question was where to find a good, reliable brothel.

The first thing Burney did on reaching Paris – recovered from his nauseating Channel crossing – was to visit a tailor to order a suit in the French style: silk trimmed with lace. Paris brought out gaiety in every visitor. Even the usually curmudgeonly Samuel Johnson bought white stockings and a new 'French-made wig of handsome construction'. Others bought two-tone velvet suits, solitaire neckpieces, diamond buckles and Brussels lace. Horace Walpole, for example, threw himself into a 'cauldron with tailors, periwig makers, snuff-box-wrights, milliners'. He said he came out quite new, 'with everything but youth'. Yet Paris made his spirits 'indecently juvenile' and he found that dancing the minuet made his gout better. Tobias Smollett noted 'total metamorphosis', but everyone agreed that Parisian tailors were cheats and not to be trusted. Still, the English have a curious attitude towards the French, both despising their 'foppishness' and wanting to emulate it.

The story of HS1

From 1994 the problem immediately became one of how to connect the Tunnel to London. In its early years of operating from Waterloo, Eurostar was hobbled in Britain by sharing track with slow commuter trains. It lurched, crawled and (often) stopped through south London and Kent: a travesty of its wasted potential. Now it is set free. Suddenly the map of Europe is to be redrawn and our concepts of travel refreshed. A revolution in travelling behaviour is promised, but realizing this was an epic of fearsome complexity: as if Dante or Milton had been called upon to describe the management of infrastructure. But it was more than digging and politicking. It was about financial management, quality-control processes, safety regimes, scrupulous environmental husbandry, tact, politics, diplomacy and bloody-mindedness.

A touching photograph taken on 24 May 1862 shows the celebrities of the day, including William Ewart Gladstone, riding in cattletrucks on a trial run of London's brand new Metropolitan Railway. Twelve years later, in his marvellous fantasy *The Hunting of the Snark*, Lewis Carroll wrote: 'They threatened its life with a railway share; /They charmed it with smiles and soap.' Gladstone and his fellow travellers were not, if the photograph's glum aspect is anything to go by, charmed with smiles and soap, but they may well have had shares in the railway. It was the first subway ride ever, a momentous incident in the urban adventure. HS1 is its successor.

The last conventional train to leave Barlow's magnificent shed at St Pancras before work began was HST powercar number 43073, the 23.40 Midland Mainline service to Derby, on 19 April 2004. Then an astonishing transformation took place. The first Eurostar to leave the new St Pancras was powercar 3001, 'Tread Lightly', at 11.03 on 14 November 2007. Indeed, 14 November is a curiously resonant date. On this day in 1940, in a less positive symbol of European relations, the Luftwaffe devastated Coventry. Now we see things differently.

Genuine European rail travel is now a reality; we can finally enjoy the New Age of the Train.

Above Celebrities of the day enjoying a proving trial on the world's first underground railway, London's Metropolitan Line, in 1862.

Right The last Midland Mainline train leaves the old St Pancras station, 19 April 2004.

Opposite Eurostar is a symbol of optimism and progress. Its design successfully glamorizes the technology.

TRACI
TUNNI
TRAIN
TERMI

'The rail was never meant to be an object of
beauty, but its cross-section has all the elegance
of fine typography.' Brian Hayes

At 300 kilometres per hour,
Eurostar's slick profile is
a matter of aerodynamic
penetration, not a cosmetic
nose job.

When British Rail and SNCF agreed on a Channel Tunnel in 1981, the
assumption, at least in Britain, was that the existing nineteenth-century rail
track to London from Folkestone, Kent, would be an entirely adequate carrier
for the imminent high-speed Trans-Manche Super Trains. What doubts there
were focused on capacity rather than speed, perhaps revealing an idiosyncratic
national trait: to a certain sort of British person, speed suggests an ungentlemanly
sort of urgency. Only in 1987, with excavations busy under water and the tunnel
portal dug into the Cretaceous chalk near Folkestone, were consultants called in
to consider new routes from the Tunnel to the centre of London. Managing the
sometimes conflicting priorities of capacity and speed while establishing a viable
route was the first achievement of what was becoming known as the Channel
Tunnel Rail Link (CTRL). The first part of the CTRL comprised the 74 kilometres

of 'Section 1' from the Channel Tunnel portal at Cheriton to Fawkham Junction, where it connected with the existing railway for its onward route to Waterloo International. When it opened on 28 September 2003, Section 1 was Britain's first new inter-urban route in a century and the only line anywhere in the country certificated for trains travelling at 300 kilometres per hour. Four years before the whole of High Speed 1 (HS1) was completed, this track took twenty minutes off the London–Paris journey. HS1 became a reality when 'Section 2' went live. Section 2 is the urban part of HS1, consisting of 38 kilometres of track threading its way around and beneath London. It reduces the international transit time by an additional fifteen minutes and provides a welcome increase in railway capacity into central London.

The political challenges

But although HS1 can be described succinctly, there was nothing simple about building it. Sections 1 and 2 were achieved after difficulty and perturbation. In fact, it could almost be said that problems and disputes are traditional in all major infrastructure projects. Although the railways are one of the defining achievements of the Victorian era, the same era's greatest art critic and social moralizer, John Ruskin, was not altogether persuaded that they made a positive contribution to civilization. It was Ruskin's peers who made and laid the tracks that compressed time and space – in fact, making modern high-consumption capitalism possible – but he did not always appreciate the democratic benefits of the railway. In his autobiography, *Praeterita* (1885–89), Ruskin wrote of the railways in Derbyshire: 'There was a rocky valley between Buxton and Bakewell … divine as the vale of Tempe; you might have seen the gods there morning and evening … Apollo and the sweet Muses of the Light … . You enterprised a railroad … you blasted rocks away … . And now, every fool in Buxton can be at Bakewell in half an hour, and every fool in Bakewell in Buxton.'

More positive views were sounded by the writer Sir Walter Scott, who said the train brought his ancestral home at Abbotsford on the River Tweed in the Scottish Borders conveniently close to his house in Hampstead, north London, and allowed him to say for the first time to almost anybody he knew, anywhere in the British Isles, 'Will you dine with us quietly tomorrow?' Thomas Arnold, one-time headmaster of Rugby School, also thought the railways brought benefits to society: 'I rejoice to see it, and to think that feudality is gone forever; it is so great a blessing to think that any one evil is really extinct.' Because of HS1 we can now, like Sir Walter Scott, invite people in Paris, Cologne and Brussels to dinner in Britain.

The Prime Minister at the time of the Channel Tunnel's planning, Mrs Thatcher, with a contrariness we can now recognize as characteristic, had been arguing for a road link. The French, by contrast, were more willing to embrace the collective solution of the train, although they acknowledged that the road tunnel was a future 'possibility'. Most of the proprietary technology of high-speed rail was in fact French in origin.

The potential benefits of direct high-speed rail travel to Continental Europe were by no means universally perceived in Britain in the late 1980s. Backbench Tories threatened rebellion. The MP for Dover fussed about economic regeneration in northern France instead of southern England. The Scottish National Party called it an 'election bribe'. One northern Labour MP objected to spending billions on merely 'digging a hole in the ground' rather than on schools. The Labour MP Andrew Faulds called the whole exercise 'expensive, unnecessary and vulnerable'.

Predictably, excitable tabloid newspapers went rabble-rousing about the prospect, as they saw it, of a new railway cutting through the Garden of England

like a demented strimmer handled by megalomaniac Frenchmen smelling of garlic. The ghost of the 27th Earl of Crawford and Balcarres, an early dissenter who in 1929 had warned of the terrible threat from French nudity and German homosexuality should there be a fixed link to Europe, hovered in editorials. 'Daggers were aimed at the heart of Kent!' 'Jobs would be drawn away from Scotland and the North-east.' The transport specialist Sir Colin Buchanan, in a stirring rearguard action, voiced doubts about the very idea of the tunnel carrying traffic of any sort. In the *Evening Standard* the socially minded journalist Paul Barker much preferred a high-speed line to Peterborough and Milton Keynes, although others warned that this might not bring the same cosmopolitan associative benefits – at least in terms of culture and gastronomy – as a high-speed line to Paris.

In the same newspaper, property correspondent Mira Bar-Hillel confidently claimed that a new track could never be built against so much public opposition. Public meetings started in 1988 and hostile newspaper cartoons began appearing at about the same time. Scarlet-faced colonels waved sticks. While the Conservative Party's advertising agency, Saatchi & Saatchi, advised British Rail on presentation styles and skills – in the words of *Private Eye*, 'to make the people of Kent think more positively about the loss of their homes' – other experts got to work on newspaper-friendly acronyms and abbreviations. When it was still intended to burrow the route under south-east London, PEARL (Peckham Against the Rail Link) argued about the blight on local property. These protests can be understood in terms of one of the significant states of consciousness in Mrs Thatcher's Britain: 'Nimbyism', NIMBY being an acronym of 'Not In My Back Yard'. To be a Nimby was to participate in a hypocritical dilemma: economic progress is a good thing, as long as it does not compromise one's own convenience, well-being, property portfolio or view from the garden.

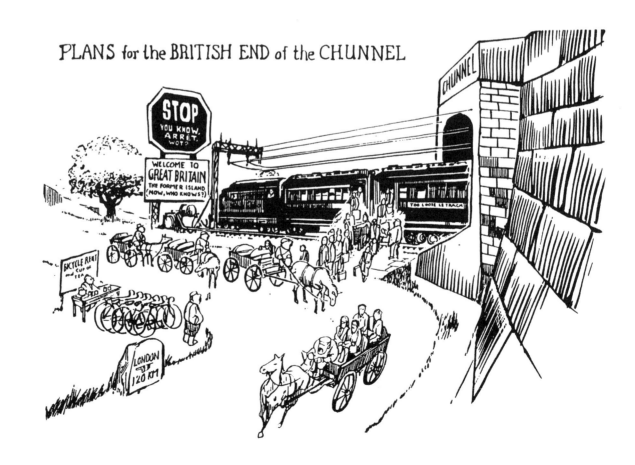

Opposite and this page
Popular anticipation of the
Channel Tunnel was in
Britain generally negative.
Cartoonists (clockwise from
right: Gaskill in *The Sun*,
Matt in the *Daily Telegraph*,
Danziger in the *Christian
Science Monitor* and
Wheeler in *The Independent*)
played on ideas of
insularity, backwardness
and absurdity.

Pages 50–51 The
Thurrock Viaduct.

'Not in my back yard' was a phrase coined in 1988 by Nicholas Ridley when
he was Secretary of State for the Environment, to describe local opposition to the
building and development boom of the late 1980s. It was the subject of a Centre for
Policy Studies paper written in 1990 by Richard Ehrman, one-time special advisor
to the Secretary of State for Employment ('Nimbyism – The Disease and the Cure',
Policy Study No. 117, Centre for Policy Studies). Unfortunately, Ridley's credentials
as an advocate of the free market in the world of property and development were
besmirched when he became a Nimby himself as he tried to protect the views from
his property in the Cotswolds. But the questions raised by Nimbyism are profound:
exactly what sort of development do we want and where exactly do we want it? For
many people the answer is indeed 'not in my back yard'. The national planning
system as defined in 1947 gave planning control to local authorities, thereby
serving local interests better than national ones. 'Nimbyism', Ehrman writes, 'is
fuelled by resentment that those adversely affected by development often suffer
the inconvenience without sharing the benefit.' One of the great successes of the
CTRL's early years was to manage Nimbyism effectively despite influential, vocal
and persistent opposition, and to address real concerns where possible.

Although civic responsibilities rather than personal property interests were
almost certainly involved, it was Paul Barker who, in an article in the *Evening
Standard* (9 March 1989), provided the *locus classicus* of Nimbyism. He wrote:
'The rail link will make things worse. We shall have extra millions of arrivals and
departures from the crowded platforms of Waterloo and King's Cross. The roads
in every direction will clog. Hoteliers, drawing their staff from among temporary
Spanish or Portuguese or Greeks, will flourish. No one else will.'

As a result, long before the construction challenges of HS1, there were
perhaps even greater obstacles in public relations and local politics. It is said
that the big problem in building a tunnel is not in the excavation, but in getting
stale air out and fresh air in. That is an engineer's perspective, but it also works
as a metaphor for all the early arguments involved in getting HS1 off, along and
under the ground.

In building HS1 the big challenge was persuading people that it could be done without defacing Kent and disrupting the county's entire population. While the French could serve compulsory purchase orders on rural communities and so build a dead-straight track across flat arable land, the historic and agriculturally valuable county of Kent is full of key marginal political constituencies. So a boggling bureaucracy of consultation and community liaison arose. Just as high-speed rail lines raise suspicions in certain quarters, so too do building works, especially when they are so ambitious, even unprecedented.

A publication by the Confederation of British Industry, *Trade Routes to the Future* (1989), contained a paper by M. Callery, originally presented to the Parliamentary Scientific Committee, entitled 'Why it takes ten years to build a road in Britain'. The answer – most of which could also be applied to building railways – is the extraordinarily elaborate series of planning processes, from 'inclusion in the preparation pool' to the start of construction, involving public consultation and inquiries, publications and decisions by the Secretary of State.

Public consultation (see page 58) was the big task in the early days of HS1, requiring the full support of the engineering, environmental and property teams. Accordingly, a technically precise definition of 'consultation' was evolved: 'an intention on the part of the project group to learn of local information and concerns as well as preparedness to improve the design using the information gained'. In pursuit of their agreement to a high-speed line, sceptics in Kent were taken for a ride by SNCF on the Atlantique branch of the French Ligne à Grande Vitesse between Paris and Tours. So impressed were they that one group dropped its resistance.

And it was with a view to securing both the practice of good citizenship and the perception of it among opponents that a new Code of Construction Practice was developed with local authorities, covering such diverse aspects as the control of lorries on the roads and the protection of wildlife habitats. Where works might involve road closures, the Highways Agency distributed warning brochures at the Channel Tunnel terminal, petrol stations and ferry terminals. There was an unusually high level of information given to the public: names and contact numbers of individuals accountable, whether contractor, project manager or client, were posted at site entrances. Contractors had their own community relations representatives, and schools were encouraged to adopt the

ferocious tunnel-boring machines churning the subterranean geology and give them appealing names. The whole of the CTRL's communications programme in its campaign for the hearts and minds of the people of Kent, Essex and London became a model for the government's Code of Practice for disseminating information on major infrastructure projects, published in 1999.

In village halls, the aim of the champions of the CTRL was to achieve constructive and honest dialogue. But it cannot be said that 'constructive and honest dialogue' necessarily led to efficient decision-making. A comedically complex graphic of obfuscatory and layered responsibilities and objectives was published for internal consumption. It showed a Draft Consultation Report, Introductions, Background Notes, Executive Summaries and the Main Report of the Consultation Exercise. These were backed up by edited versions of

PROPERTY ACQUISITION

The scale of the property acquisition can only be judged by the sheer number of transactions that had to be completed before work could even begin on the new railway. More than 6500 properties had to be purchased in whole or part, affecting more than 12,300 parties. Not only were 110 kilometres of new railway to be built, but also some 65 kilometres of new roads and 50 kilometres of diverted services had to be accommodated on land purchased by the project. This involved people's homes and livelihoods more than any other aspect of the CTRL, and so each property presented its own challenges. The spectre of disaffected property owners chaining themselves to bulldozers was not something that those working on the project wished to see, or, in the event, caused.

Once the Channel Tunnel Rail Link Act of Parliament had been given Royal Assent, in December 1996, the property division began the complex task of obtaining all the necessary land. A dedicated team of property professionals was set up as part of the project team, and with the commitment and continuity of staff managing all aspects of the transactions from initial discussion to acquisition and disposal of any surplus, all the land required was obtained without any delay to the planned construction works. It has been said that this was the largest programme of property purchase undertaken by any single organization since the Second World War, but the exercise was conducted peaceably with very little recourse to law.

computer-aggregated summaries, reports on responses to consultations and appendices with verbatim notes on consultation meetings; a great deal of space in the report was reserved for options that had been considered but set aside.

The key design objectives for the new railway were: first, to use existing transport channels, if at all possible; and second, to hide the tracks. By 1988 four major routes through south-east London and Kent had been identified as possibilities:

1. Sidcup–Snodland–Medway Viaduct–Charing–North Ashford
2. Bromley–Swanley–Longfield–Snodland–Medway Viaduct–Charing–North Ashford
3. Bromley–Swanley–Marden–Pluckley–South Ashford
4. Bromley–Swanley–tunnels–Tonbridge–Marden–Pluckley–South Ashford

There followed an exhausting and complex sequence of structuring and restructuring, alignments, yet more consultations, realignments and politicking. At one stage there were options that totalled more than 1000 kilometres, for actual requirements of only 109 kilometres. That statistic illustrates the enormity of the political processes involved in providing high-speed train travel.

But in October 1991 the then transport minister, Malcolm Rifkind, recommended a north-easterly approach to the capital from the River Medway, promoted by the civil engineers Arup. This change of direction was not welcomed by British Rail, which had spent a great deal of time at the behest of the Department of Transport developing a southerly approach route to Waterloo and King's Cross. British Rail's proposals would always involve the best transport solution, as it would not benefit from incidental development; but Arup's proposal involved the redevelopment of the East Thames corridor, making it more attractive. Three levels of 'sifting' or 'optioneering' took place during 1992–93, and in April 1994 the final route options were presented to the government, to be considered by Parliament during the next two years. A competition was meanwhile run to find a private-sector promoter with the expertise and financial capability necessary for the building and running of the proposed new railway, to be given the right to manage the UK part of Eurostar and an interest in the development plans at King's Cross, St Pancras and Stratford. Nine international consortia bid for the opportunity, and on 29 February 1996 the concession was granted to the London & Continental Railways (LCR) consortium. The CTRL Act was passed on 18 December 1996, providing the consortium with the legal powers to purchase the necessary property interests and construct and operate the new railway.

The commercial challenges

Successfully constructing the UK's first major railway for more than a century was always going to be difficult. At the beginning of 1998 there was growing concern that LCR's traffic projections and the revenue predictions based on them were unrealistic, following optimistic passenger forecasts (even before anyone had really heard of low-cost air travel). It had always been assumed that the UK part of the Eurostar business would generate extra funds, which would cover both the building of and borrowings to finance the construction of the CTRL. With passenger numbers much lower than forecast, Eurostar (UK) was consuming and would continue to consume LCR's limited cash. LCR was forced to put forward an alternative financing proposal, which it presented to John Prescott (Secretary of State for the Environment, Transport and the Regions, as well as Deputy Prime Minister). At first appalled by the proposal, Prescott realized that LCR was requesting an extra £1.2 billion of government money. On 28 January 1998 he announced to the House of Commons that LCR would be unable to raise the finance for the railway. In order to be given

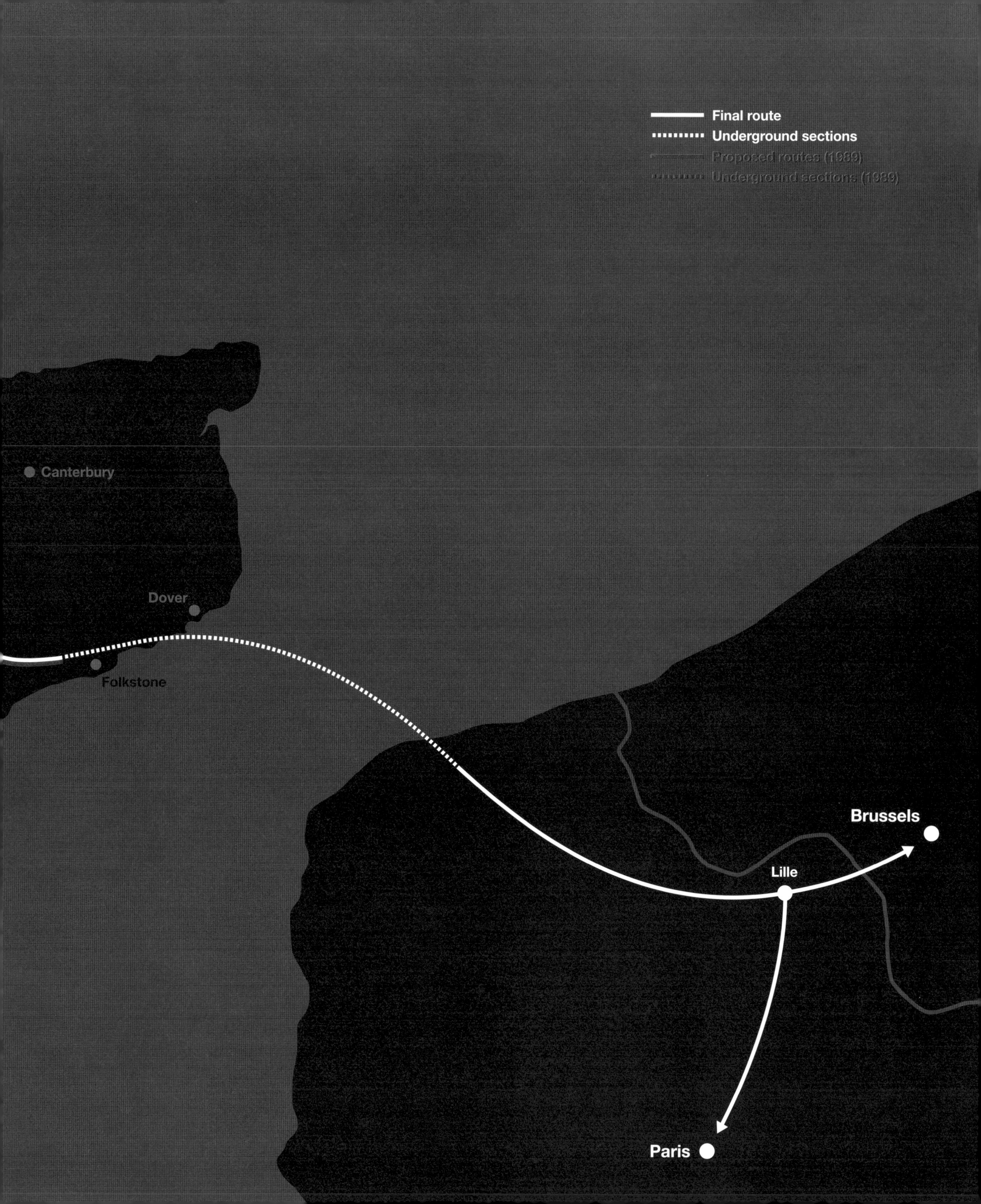
Final route
Underground sections
Proposed routes (1989)
Underground sections (1989)
Canterbury
Dover
Folkstone
Brussels
Lille
Paris

PUBLIC CONSULTATION

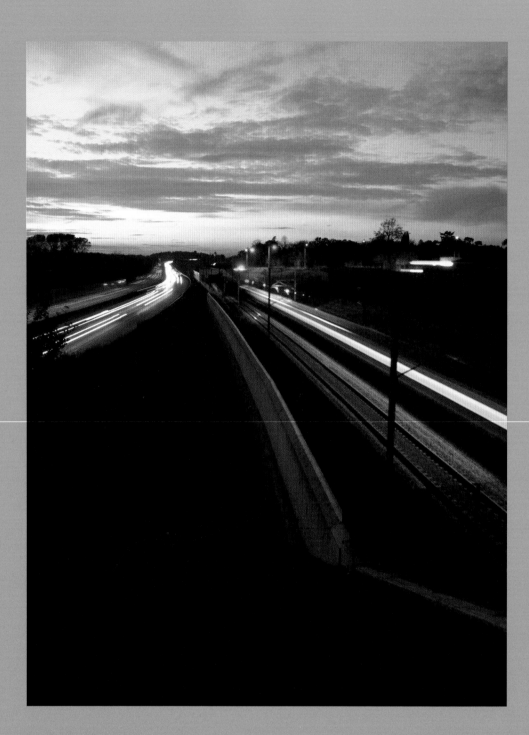

One of the many problems of HS1 was the public concern caused by the uncertainty of the programme, timescale and impact. Early plans, published with the best of intentions by the promoters seeking to consult and win over the affected communities, had the opposite effect. The people of Kent already opposed the Channel Tunnel and the extra traffic it was sure to generate; a high-speed railway slashing through the Garden of England was a concept too far.

Experienced pressure groups and established parish councils formed the first line of defence, and soon made their feelings clear, challenging the proposals with a greater knowledge of the territory than those on the 'other side' could hope to assemble. The residents' objections could only be answered once the plans had developed further. With the railway in operation the episode is now seen as a good example of what can be done to address concerns of environmental impact and dislocation of communities.

In London the problems were different, as were the people: there were no established parochial organizations or local community groups, so it was for the residents to form action groups to put their point across, together with the local planning authority. The consequences (subsidence and ground-borne noise and vibration) of constructing large-diameter tunnels under many thousands of residential properties were high on the agenda. The affected communities ranged across east London, from recent immigrants with little understanding of English or the legal protections in place, to the social elite of Islington with the means to call on experts and legal advisors. Community relations teams and – once work had been authorized – contractors held regular meetings to reassure the public, with satisfactory results.

Deputy Prime Minister John Prescott was the most senior political champion of the Channel Tunnel Rail Link.

a second chance, LCR needed to find supporters from the private sector with the funds to construct the railway and support Eurostar (UK). And so in June the government agreed to LCR's revised proposals: that the CTRL would be constructed in two sections; that Railtrack would underwrite the construction of Section 1 (from the Channel Tunnel to Southfleet in north Kent), with the option to do the same with Section 2 (Southfleet to St Pancras); that a consortium of National Express, SNCF, SNCB and British Airways would be invited to take on Eurostar (UK); and, most significantly, that such a project was impossible without government support. This last proposal resulted in the announcement that the government would guarantee a series of LCR bond issues to raise £3.75 billion.

The project continued to plan. But by 2001 it had become apparent that before giving the go-ahead for Section 2, the government would require further private-sector capital to underwrite the risk. In this adversity, Bechtel, LCR's founder shareholder, led by its Executive Vice President John Carter (also non-executive director of LCR), put forward an innovative solution: what became known as a cost over-run protection programme (COPP) for the construction of Section 2. The programme was a unique risk-sharing idea involving LCR, RLE, Bechtel and some of the world's largest re-insurance companies: AIG, Swiss Re, Zurich Re and General. The incentive was strong for all parties involved in the construction of Section 2 to avoid cost over-runs. The insurers were attracted because the parties managing the project were themselves at risk, providing a firewall of protection before the insurers became exposed. Although for many the COPP was expensive, it shared the risk to an extent that the government approved the completion of the CTRL.

On 2 April 2001 John Prescott signed an agreement at St Pancras Chambers allowing work to begin on Section 2 on 2 July at Stratford. Later that year – well before the completion of Section 1 – the government's decision to put Railtrack into administration allowed LCR to recover the interest it had given to Railtrack in 1998 and put back together the two sections of HS1. It was necessary to refinance some of the debt guaranteed by Railtrack for the construction of Section 1, but this was greatly preferable to the larger cost of financing Railtrack's investment.

Following the successful completion of Section 2 in October 2007, the COPP was closed without having resulted in any claim against Bechtel or the insurers. As a whole, HS1 involved remarkably few commercial disputes, a tribute to the strong partnership between managers and contractors, the professionalism of the negotiators and the practice of prompt action to resolve problems and avoid delays.

The engineering challenges

After the CTRL Act was passed, protests diminished to the point that at John Prescott's sod-cutting photo-call at Medway, Kent, in October 1998, there were no angry interruptions of any sort. The Nimbys had been quietened. The then Deputy Prime Minister, magnificent in hard hat, stood next to a sign that pointed one way to 'London and the Regions' and another way to 'Amsterdam, Brussels, Cologne, Paris'.

Politically speaking, the route of HS1 passes through the following local authorities: Camden, Islington, Hackney, Newham, Barking and Dagenham, Havering, Thurrock, Dartford, Gravesham, Medway, Tonbridge and Malling, Maidstone, Ashford and Shepway. Topographically speaking, from St Pancras the route passes the connection to the West Coast mainline near Camden Town before entering the first 7.5-kilometre section of the London Tunnel on its way to the new Stratford International station in north-east London, the transport hub of the 2012 Olympics. Terry Hill, chairman of Arup, has said that the creation of Stratford station was about as straightforward as 'inserting Tottenham Court Road [25 metres deep] into a flood plain'. The route then enters the second

ARCHAEOLOGY

The construction of HS1 provided a unique opportunity to investigate thousands of years of change and development in the landscapes of Kent, Essex and London. An extraordinarily rich and diverse array of sites, features and deposits was discovered during the extensive programme of archaeological works, which started years before construction itself began. Discoveries range from a 400,000-year-old elephant to Second World War pillboxes.

Saltwood

The remains of five Bronze Age burial mounds were found here in a dig measuring nearly 1 kilometre in length, one of the largest on HS1. The same site was also used for over 200 Anglo-Saxon burials more than 2000 years later, during the sixth and seventh centuries AD. A wealth of grave goods was also found, including weapons, glass vessels, bronze bowls and a superlative gold, garnet and blue-glass brooch (1).

Parsonage Farm

A moated, stone-built medieval hall and its outbuildings were found near Westwell in Kent. The high status of its thirteenth- and fourteenth-century inhabitants was revealed by their fine pottery and jewellery, and the bones of animals on which they dined.

Sandway Road, Harrietsham

A campsite of Mesolithic nomads was recorded, and 11,000 pieces of flint debris – evidence of their tool-making – were found, left in the hollows in which they worked.

Blue Bell Hill

At the entrance to the new tunnel under the North Downs an early Neolithic longhouse was discovered, buried under nearly 5 metres of soil (2). Buildings of the first prehistoric farmers are rare, and this is the first time one has been found in Kent.

Cuxton

A small Anglo-Saxon cemetery containing just thirty-five burials – some containing weapons, including spears and shields – was excavated. Cut into chalk and overlooking the River Medway, the burial mounds and graves would have been visible across a wide area.

Ebbsfleet

• *Palaeoloxodon antiquus* (4), an elephant, roamed the valley 400,000 years ago along with rhinoceros, aurochs and deer. Early humans also left their traces there; hundreds of their flint tools were recorded, as well as debris.

• The Roman town of Vagniacis ('the estate by the marsh') was probably an earlier place of pilgrimage. Adding to the temples previously discovered, work for HS1 identified another temple and, more importantly, a major sanctuary complex focused on the springs.

• A watermill was discovered beneath the deposits of the River Ebbsfleet. Dendrochronology (tree-ring dating) of one of the planks in the mill identified the exact felling date of the tree as some time in the spring of AD 692, making the mill one of the earliest of its kind in the UK.

Stratford Box

The construction of the kilometre-long Stratford station box provided evidence for prehistoric, Roman and later activity in the Lea Valley.

St Pancras burial ground

At St Pancras part of a post-medieval graveyard lay beneath the tracks of the Midland Mainline railway. Investigations during construction work gave historians a fascinating insight into the lives of its occupants at a time of great change.

THE BUILT ENVIRONMENT

The route of HS1 through the populated countryside of Kent affected eleven historic structures, requiring varied solutions: most were recorded, dismantled and re-erected in new locations as homes and businesses; some were recorded and demolished, their most important features salvaged and given to museums; and one house was slid to a new site away from the line.

Talbot House

This timber-framed house, dating from about 1450, was dismantled and rebuilt on the opposite side of Sellindge village. The opportunity was taken to remove Victorian brick cladding to reveal its original construction (3).

Bridge House

This timber-framed, stone-fronted house at Mersham, built and developed between the sixteenth and the eighteenth centuries, stood uncomfortably close to the new railway cutting. Rather than dismantle and reconstruct it, engineers decided to slide it 50 metres up the slope, away from the railway and the disruptive construction activity (5). The 450-ton structure was underpinned with a concrete ring beam and the whole jacked up and moved on rails lubricated with about a ton of grease. It took eight hours to move the structure over a period of two days.

Yonsea Farm

Designed by John Nash's pupil George Stanley Repton, Yonsea Farm (6) was built as a model farm in the early nineteenth century to put to full use new theories of agricultural improvement. Before work began on this part of HS1, the whole farm complex was recorded, dismantled and removed to the South of England Rare Breeds Centre at Woodchurch, near Tenterden, to be re-erected and given a new lease of life as a training and educational centre.

Brockton Farm

The seventeenth-century farmhouse yielded a curious deposit. Three mummified cats (7), a selection of leather shoes, clothes and personal objects were found behind a studwork partition on the first floor. It is thought that such 'spiritual middens' were intended to keep out evil spirits.

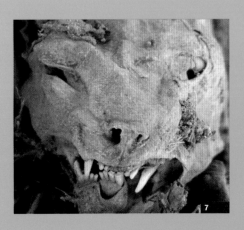

Below, opposite and pages 64–65 The Medway Viaduct is a balanced cantilever design. Built using 'push-launch' techniques, it is the longest high-speed rail bridge in the world. It runs dead straight past the sinuous M2 motorway.

portion of the London Tunnel, 10 kilometres long, before emerging again at Dagenham. There is a freight connection at Ripple Lane in Barking, then the track passes along the edge of the Thames marshes and through the industrial areas of east London before spearing its way under the QEII bridge and the M25. Diving under the River Thames, it emerges in Kent, passing through Ebbsfleet International station with its park-and-ride car parks, racing the A2/M2 highway and skimming the River Medway on a stunning viaduct. The 3-kilometre North Downs Tunnel follows, then the route enters Ashford International station, and thereafter – whoosh! – it travels into the Channel Tunnel, underground, underwater, into France. All in less than an hour from St Pancras. Even John Ruskin might have been impressed.

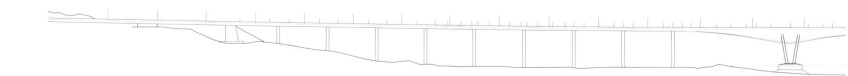

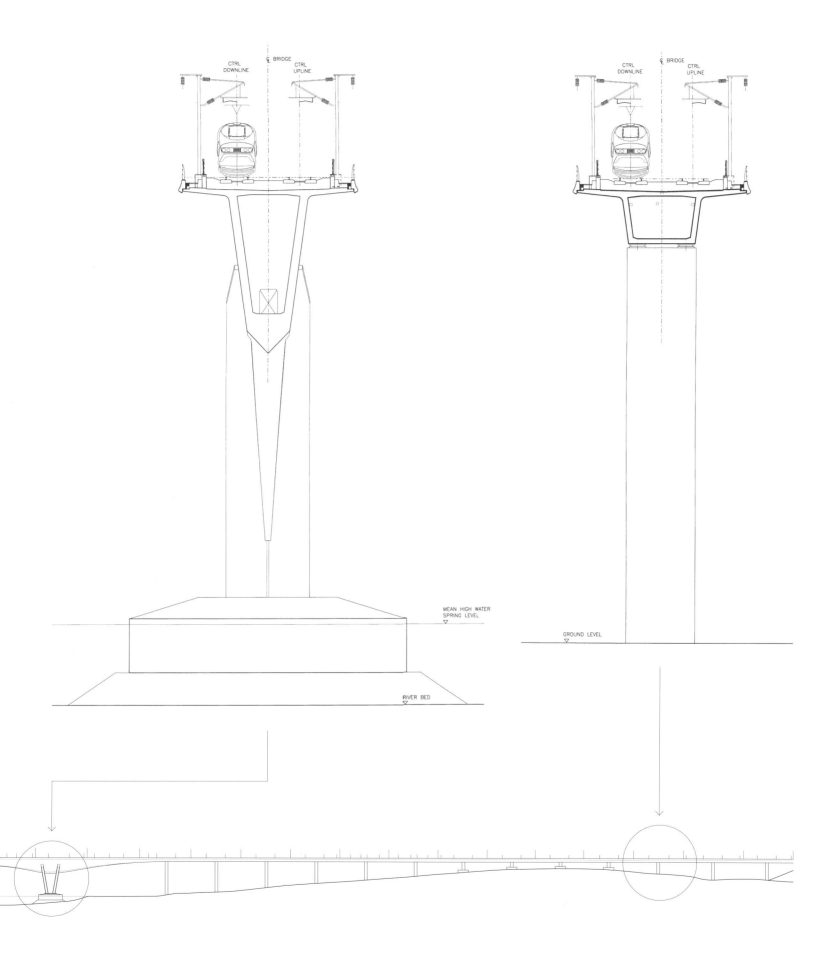

CTRL DOWNLINE ℄ BRIDGE CTRL UPLINE

CTRL DOWNLINE ℄ BRIDGE CTRL UPLINE

MEAN HIGH WATER SPRING LEVEL ▽

RIVER BED ▽

GROUND LEVEL ▽

50 KM
DOWN TRACK

Opposite A Eurostar
enters the 3.2-kilometre-
long North Downs Tunnel.

Below The Medway
Viaduct gives high-speed
travellers a different
perspective of the view
enjoyed by J.M.W. Turner.

The Medway Viaduct

There are two structures that visually define the creation of the Channel Tunnel Rail Link. St Pancras International is one of them; the award-winning Medway Viaduct is the other. The longest high-speed rail bridge in the world, and a beautifully balanced piece of construction, it is technically Contract 350 of the CTRL, and a crucial part of the project (until the Medway was successfully crossed, the completion of the entire line was at risk). Civil-engineering construction took place between October 1998 and November 2001 and was the work of a consortium of Miller, Dumez-GTM and Beton Monierbau. The viaduct, which crosses the river after which it is named close to Rochester, Kent, is, in fact, three different bridges: two approach spans and a central section. Essentially a push-launch on an enormous scale, part of the beauty of the viaduct (for the engineers, at least) lies in the combination of bold and innovative techniques with which it was built.

The central span was constructed as a balanced cantilever. The piers were built up from river level, and the decks (comprising thirty-three sections) supported by the piers were built out simultaneously in opposite directions, so that the overall balance of the structure was maintained. The two approach spans were literally pushed into place out over the water: the deck was cast in sections and progressively edged towards the piers by massive hydraulic rams. 'It's magnificent in its simplicity,' says Mike Glover, a director of Arup. 'It feels as though someone has really made an effort to achieve elegance.' The viaduct is a fine example of that rare engineering triumph: a design that integrates structural efficiency, 'constructability' and aesthetics. Passengers have outstanding views over the Medway valley in a cruelly short, fifteen-second snapshot as the Eurostar races at 300 kilometres per hour across the 1.25-kilometre viaduct.

The North Downs Tunnel, bridges, crossings and stations

The North Downs Tunnel was more straightforward than other tunnels on the project (see pages 90–100), but at 3.2 kilometres long it was still a notable engineering achievement, passing 100 metres underneath Blue Bell Hill, 6 kilometres north of Maidstone in Kent. As with many of the tunnels, bridges and crossings of HS1, its alignment was fixed by the constraints of the CTRL legislation. Its depth was determined by an altogether different force: the balance between the requirement for high speed and the economics of keeping the tunnel as short as possible.

Excavation began at both ends using giant tracked drills and excavators. As soon as a short section of the profile had been cut, Shotcrete (a type of spray-applied concrete) was applied to the chalk. Then came steel reinforcements, followed by more coats of Shotcrete. A cast-in-place concrete shell provides a secondary lining. The tunnel bore is sufficiently generous that two Eurostars can pass within it at 300 kilometres per hour without aerodynamic incident. The tunnel is also provided with passenger evacuation walkways and emergency lighting in case of train failure.

Planning this tunnel involved unprecedentedly detailed deep-level research, exhaustive 'value-engineering workshops' and painstaking design. The result was that when the tunnel was completed, six months early and £5 million under-budget, 21,000 cubic metres less chalk had been excavated and 35,000 cubic metres less concrete used than the engineers had envisaged.

Other major engineering works on HS1 are the A2/M2 crossings, the freight loops and the stations. Kent County Council and the Highways Agency had to be assured that the crossings would cause minimal disruption to existing communities and the continuous traffic. The A2 crossing at Pepper Hill, south-west of Gravesend, used the cut-and-cover method of tunnelling, in an operation

HS1 passenger services travel through Kent in an uninterrupted straight, but the railway also incorporates 'freight loops' so that goods can be manoeuvred. These are at Charing Heath (top) and Singlewell (bottom).

that took place in stages so that no fewer than three lanes of the trunk road were open at any one time.

Galley Hill Road and the North Kent line, 2.5 kilometres north of Pepper Hill, presented another obstacle. Here chalk quarrying had, over the years, produced an extraordinary landscape with strange parallel 'spines' supporting local road and rail routes. These chalk walls lay in the path of HS1. Mike Glover explains how the road was undercut: 'We diverted the road on to a temporary embankment, installed foundations and abutments down through the chalk spine, cast the bridge deck on top of the spine and finally mined the chalk underneath to create a bridge, returning the road to its original alignment.' Even more exciting was a 'bridge slide' under the existing railway line, carried out, under RLE's direction, by joint-venture contractor Hochtief/Norwest Holst. This involved building an entire bridge off-site. At the same time, short tunnels were driven through the base of the chalk spine, allowing the preparation of subfoundations. Then, over fifty-two hours, starting on a Friday night, the whole bridge, including its abutments and central pier (a total weight of more than 9100 tons), was slid on rails into the gap created as the remaining chalk was ripped out. The fit was perfect.

There are two freight loops on Section 1 of HS1, at Charing Heath/Lenham and at Singlewell, near Gravesend. Each loop, 2.5 kilometres long, is a sort of railway lay-by so slow-moving or defective trains can be quite literally sidetracked. The length of the loop was determined by calculating the combined length of two 750-metre-long freight trains and adding their braking distances.

A mere seventeen minutes along HS1 from St Pancras International is Ebbsfleet International station in Kent, built on a brownfield site of 50 hectares and the largest surface development of the CTRL after St Pancras itself. Like Stratford International (see pages 107–12), it accommodates Eurostar and

CONSTRUCTION AT ASHFORD

The High Speed 1 tunnel runs beneath major roads near Ashford station. Part of a row of terraced houses was demolished to make way for it.

The cut-and-cover tunnel and viaduct at Ashford were the most demanding civil-engineering tasks on Section 1. HS1 had to pass under a major road junction as well as beneath the old Ashford–Maidstone railway and then over the lines to Canterbury (and all this while business continued as usual in the town and its railway station). Sewers and infrastructure for other utilities had to be diverted. An industrial park and a section of the terraced houses on Godinton Road were demolished. This work was organized in isolated pockets to minimize disruption to the old railway town, where the South Eastern Railway had built its works in 1843.

domestic services. The site is 2.6 kilometres long and contains six tracks: two international and two domestic platforms on the main CTRL, plus two extra domestic platforms on a new connection to the existing North Kent line. Non-stopping trains travelling at 225 kilometres per hour use through tracks.

Like Stratford, the station is a modern construction of steel and glass, designed for transparency of function and aesthetic pleasure from both inside and outside. The station building itself sits on top of an enormous steel-and-concrete 'raft' straddling the tracks, offering dramatic views of the trains and surrounding area for waiting passengers. The roof is a semi-transparent membrane glazed with 2200 square metres of glass, bringing in dazzling levels of natural light. This is billed as the ultimate park-and-ride station, strategically placed just off the A2/M2 trunk road and close to the M25 motorway, serving a

Pages 70–71 The approach to Ebbsfleet: High Speed 1's domestic services will help create a new town in this run-down part of north Kent.

This page and opposite
Ebbsfleet International – the ultimate park-and-ride station – opened on 29 January 2008.

catchment area of more than 10 million people. Initially, 5000 car-parking spaces have been provided; eventually there will be room for up to 9000 cars. Of all unlikely places, neglected, run-down, depressed and forgotten Ebbsfleet will open Europe to new markets. A subtle shift in Euro-geography has occurred; Bluewater and the Bon Marché have not yet merged, but they have moved closer.

The intention was never that HS1 should be just Britain's first high-speed railway line. One of the main objectives was to stimulate regeneration of the Thames Gateway region, and, following the completion of Ebbsfleet International, a major new mixed-use development of light commercial and residential units will be built on worked-out quarries that once served the cement industry. A new plaza bridge has already been constructed near the station, as part of the HS1 works, to smooth the progress of regeneration. Around the station, more than 400 hectares of land have been identified for development, which is predicted to amount to 10,000 new homes (840,000 square metres of living space), offices and 25,000 new jobs by 2027.

The track and signalling

Despite the obvious and effective high technology, the railways are a keen reminder of the last century, its cultures, structures and mechanics. As the American science writer Brian Hayes says in his superb book *Infrastructure* (2006), 'the industrial style and culture of the railroads have changed remarkably little in the past few years'. Despite the drama of Japan's Shinkansen, which began running between Tokyo and Osaka on dedicated high-speed track in the mid-1960s, or the Paris–Lyon TGV service of 1981, the underlying technologies are fundamentally conventional.

The mechanics of any railway are beautifully simple. The basic concept of iron wheels running on iron rails has not changed since the 1830s. The great advantage of steel-on-steel is low rolling resistance, which makes the movement of heavier loads possible. Guided by rails, trains need no steering mechanism and their performance is limited only by concerns of comfort for passengers, who expect a smooth ride and the ability to walk up and down the carriages in safety. The measure of stability for a train is the coffee cup. The faster the train, the greater the dynamic forces (acceleration, braking and curving) generated, hence the gentle curves and shallow gradients of HS1.

HS1 still uses conventional welded rails, concrete sleepers and crushed stone ballast for the open sections of the route, but the track is set in concrete in the London and Thames tunnels. The major innovation of the current generation of high-speed lines is the very high standard of construction and maintenance of the track, providing an extremely stable and smooth running surface. Fast trains need to draw a large amount of electrical power, which is delivered by the overheard catenary system and collected by the train's pantograph. Until recently the various European countries had different electric power-supply systems, so the Eurostar train when it entered service on 14 November 1994 was designed to operate at three different voltages and with three different current-collection systems. With the gradual standardization of European railway systems, the Eurostar train now operates on 25,000 volts AC, greatly simplifying the on-board systems and improving reliability. On completion, the track itself was successively energized westwards towards St Pancras. Seamlessness of power supply was essential and so, too, was a guarantee of no electrical interference.

HS1 has been built to the International Union of Railways 'C' gauge specification, and has been constructed to comply with the European Union's Interoperability Standard. This portion of Britain's railway can thus accept the largest European trains, provided only that the International Safety Commission

Opposite Fast trains need to draw a large amount of electrical power, which is delivered by the overhead catenary system, passing here in a blur.

Above, left High Speed 1 uses conventional welded rails, concrete sleepers and crushed stone ballast.

Above, right It is impossible for a driver to read trackside signals at 300 kilometres per hour, so High Speed 1 uses Centralized Track Control.

approves the Continental trains for passage through the Channel Tunnel, as it surely will. Currently TGVs and ICEs are not able to use the Channel Tunnel without having their safety systems modified, but the Eurostars that use the tunnel are specially designed to comply with the requirements of the four railway authorities through which they pass (British, EuroTunnel, French and Belgian).

With trains running at such high speeds, it is vital that the track be kept clear of obstructions. The route is a dedicated corridor, protected by high-security systems and physical barriers. There are no level crossings on HS1 and no personnel are allowed on the track during high-speed operation.

A cross-section of HS1 rail is much the same as that of George Stephenson's Stockton–Darlington line, although it has progressively evolved. There is a head, a web and a foot. Signalling is one thing that has changed, however, in technology if not in principle. At the beginning of the railway age, the train was the fastest thing on earth. Nothing could outrun it, so safety could only be guaranteed by strictly observed timetabling. Then the electric telegraph changed the dynamic of railway communications. It is virtually impossible to read trackside signals at 300 kilometres per hour, so HS1 uses an automatic system known generically as CTC (Centralized Track Control). The signalling system, linked to the train, is an automatic train-protection system that will override the driver and brake if the train exceeds its authorized maximum speed or passes a red signal. Essentially, however, this system relies on block signalling techniques that go back to the very beginning of the railways. Block signalling divides the length of the track into sections, or blocks, and allows only one train in a block at any one time. Originally signals were set manually by trackside workers, but in 1870 the age of automation began when the track itself was conceived as an electrical circuit that the train completed as it progressed.

THE MANAGERS OF HIGH SPEED 1

HS1 was finished on time and within budget, through clear leadership and an outstanding commitment of human energy and ingenuity. Below, successive managing directors describe what it took in personal terms to make a brand-new railway.

John Armitt, a 'construction professional' and now chairman of the Olympic Delivery Authority, was managing director of Union Railways from 1993 to 1997. He piloted the project through the difficult Parliamentary consideration phase, when, over a period of two years, the locally critical arguments for and against the new railway were debated and considered by select committees in both Houses of Parliament, eventually leading to Royal Assent to the Channel Tunnel Rail Link Act. He is eloquent about the relative ease with which the French built their high-speed railway. The people of Kent did not want it in their backyard, but the people of Nord-Pas-de-Calais in northern France emphatically did want it in theirs. Armitt insists that ninety per cent of major infrastructure projects in the UK are successful, although he accepts that LCR's early (and persuasive) passenger forecasts were optimistic. He is aware of the railway's subtle relationship between technology and the environment. He deplores legislation that is a brake on progress. Japanese trains, for example, are about half the gross weight per passenger of their European equivalents, because Europeans insist on heavier bogies. It may be a presentational

stance, but for this reason Hitachi (which is supplying domestic high-speed 'Javelin' trains for HS1) claims it cannot deliver optimum performance. So, Armitt says, 'the railway cannot assume it is the natural home of the environmentalist unless it becomes more technologically advanced.' Still, Hitachi's reservations notwithstanding, Armitt summarizes HS1 as an 'international project made possible by the domestic benefits arising from the high-speed services and the regeneration of the East Thames Gateway region. This made the compelling argument to the government to invest in this, the first new mainline railway for one hundred years. The railway will be an enduring element of essential infrastructure, the benefit of which will last for generations.'

Chris Jago was appointed managing director for Section 1 by Railtrack when it undertook to provide financial support for the Channel Tunnel Rail Link project. Work started in October 1998, and Section 1 was opened to commercial traffic as scheduled in September 2003, within budget. He says: 'We delivered a successful project through the application of sound project-management and use of sophisticated risk-management techniques, where the probability of an adverse event was identified and action plans put in place.' However, despite their best endeavours drama occurred during his tenure. 'We had three exceptional rainstorms in Kent, which flooded our earthworks when the sun should have

been shining. We suffered shortages of fuel during the national fuel-tax demonstrations when fuel depots were blockaded, just when we were back on programme. Then we could not get deliveries of rail from Continental suppliers, as the wagons were seen by illegal immigrants as the ideal transport opportunity between France and the UK. The people just swarmed over the trains, and we had to suspend deliveries until adequate security could be imposed.' The difficulties were overcome and the project opened on time, following successful trial runs. This included a Eurostar train breaking the UK rail speed record at 334.7 kilometres per hour. Jago, a railway operator at heart, takes great pride in saying that 'not only did the project get completed on time, but also it has proved to be a highly reliable and high-quality construction, probably the best in the world.'

Walt Bell is an American who brought experience of global heavy construction to the project as managing director of Union Railways North from 1999 to 2003. He is generous in his regard for the achievements of the British and French engineers. 'The successful completion of this truly mega public-works project on schedule and to budget is a remarkable achievement of a kind that is virtually unheard of. Fundamentally, it is the result of the efforts of many very talented and dedicated people at all levels and disciplines. Frankly, in all my years in this business, I have never worked with an

abler team, in all areas, than this one. The team was further enabled by an ethos of partnership that was unique to the project and assisted the players to innovate and bring their talents to bear on the goals.' He identifies three key elements of the project: 'First, the exceptionally detailed and fine-tuned study and conceptual work done by Union Railways in its British Rail days set the stage for implementation without the usual remaining pile of obstacles to be resolved, as in so many major projects. Secondly, the contracting process was unique in the public-works arena: instead of using the traditional lump-sum, fixed-price method, contractors were competitively selected based on their professional and staff qualifications, innovative approaches and ability to partner.' This led to a contract with negotiated target prices and reimbursable costs backed by a 'pain/gain sharing arrangement', allowing a genuine design-and-build effort, fully integrating the contractors and producing 'a fully focused execution partnership'. Essentially, the contractors had as much at stake as the management. The third element, says Bell, 'was the quick decision-making delivered by a knowledgeable client, LCR and the open-layered management organization that it had set in place, through Union Railways to the project manager, Rail Link Engineering.'

Alan Dyke joined the Rail Link Project team in 1989, when it was still a British Rail project, becoming chief engineer and finally managing director before retiring in 2005. 'Initially British Rail was sceptical about the possibility of making a new railway, but the government needed one. Increased passenger capacity, rather than higher speed, was the objective at the time.' Dyke was there throughout the debate between British Rail's preference for a southerly route, which in terms of transport was the optimum solution, and the Arup proposal for an easterly one (the political preference, since it would almost inevitably stimulate development en route). Dyke oversaw the decision to switch the terminus from King's Cross to St Pancras. The eight-platform subterranean station originally planned below King's Cross was always an expensive option, but with the route now approaching from the east through Stratford the opportunity to reuse St Pancras became apparent. This Victorian masterpiece was both woefully under-exploited and in extremely bad condition. Not only was the St Pancras solution calculated to be several hundred million pounds cheaper than the King's Cross one, but also it immediately secured valuable cultural credentials for the entire project. It was under Dyke, too, that the civil-engineering campaign for the route was developed. 'Originally, it was intended to start in London and work towards the Channel Tunnel in a single sequence. This was seen as too ambitious by the financial backers, which by then included Railtrack, so it was decided to do the "easy" bit first and start in Kent.'

Dave Pointon was appointed managing director of Union Railways North in September 2005. That year, with the civil engineering all but complete, the project needed a railwayman to bring it to life as a fully functioning high-speed railway. Like an aircraft in a hangar, a cold, silent, dead machine, a railway is just steel and gravel until the lines are powered up. Pointon took up the challenge. 'Twenty years before the grand opening of the project I started work on the Channel Tunnel, so it was a great privilege to be asked to deliver the final piece in the rail link,' he says. He is full of admiration for the achievements of the team, knowing just what it takes to construct such major works as this. 'When I came, the heavy work had been completed with a well-motivated team in place, but moving it into an operational railway takes a different set of skills and experience. It is all about teamwork, and we have multiple systems that have to be aligned and coordinated,' he explains. 'St Pancras is awe-inspiring, a masterpiece of engineering and architecture, and the public face of the project, but the clever bits, those that deliver a safe and reliable high-speed railway, are hidden away in secure control centres. The public can be reassured that not only do St Pancras and HS1 look the business, they also deliver it!'

Below, left The Thurrock
Viaduct carries the railway
over marshy land to the
north of the River Thames.

Below, right The Medway
Viaduct.

Opposite A stylish angle
and dramatic lighting of
the Medway Viaduct show
that infrastructure can be
beautiful.

The engineering achievement

Long after the Nimbys and the archaeological excavations, it is the engineering challenges and their solutions that define the traveller's experience of HS1. But for most passengers the achievement of HS1 will be enjoyed, but not observed: a railway that works well leaves no very clear impression of itself. And while the tunnels under east London and the Thames and through the North Downs are fine engineering, they are, if not invisible, then black holes. Paradoxically, the success of the whole project – fast track, efficient signals, a calm on-board environment – may be judged by how little it intrudes on the traveller's consciousness. That is a truism accepted by the self-effacing civil engineers who ran the project, content to have achieved anonymous efficiency, but the Medway Viaduct, the most visible structure of the new railway, does provide a useful symbol of the larger poetics in play.

Any bridge, like the bicycle, is a rare example of technology with no downside. Designed to strict rules (the mechanics allow little excess) bridges are almost always pleasing. They combine the essentials of architecture: poetry and logic. The poetry comes from the romantic achievement of bringing together, against the original intention of Nature, two areas hitherto separated by river or gorge. The logic derives from the simple good sense of doing so: bridges, as well as a humane delight, are economic tools that generate traffic and prosperity and excite curiosity.

Poets have often been struck by the metaphor of the bridge. Longfellow was inspired: 'The grave itself is but a covered bridge,/ Leading from light to light, through a brief darkness!' Shakespeare sensed the deeper meaning: 'What need the bridge much broader than the flood?' Don Pedro asks in *Much Ado About Nothing*. But to answer him, that is the art of bridge-building: making a structure that exceeds bare necessity … but not by too much. The design of HS1's visible infrastructure proves that old principle that rules are an inspiration to genius, not an impediment to it.

TRACI

TUNNI

TRAIN

TERMI

EL

S

NUS

**'The phonographs of Hades in the brain
Are tunnels that re-wind themselves, and love
A burnt match skating in a urinal.'**
Hart Crane, 'The Tunnel' (1930)

Early on in the history of the railways, tunnels were part of the passengers' experience of the new form of travel. One of the very first descriptions of a dedicated railway tunnel was the one written by Charles Young in 1835. Approaching Liverpool from Manchester, he found 'a dark, black, ugly, vile abominable tunnel of 300 yards long, which has all the horrors of banishment from life – such a hole as I never wish to go through again'.

Artist, sculptor and typographer Eric Gill's account of travelling on the footplate of an old steam express captures much of the sheer untamed, visceral drama of piloting hundreds of rapidly moving tons of hot metal into a dark cavity with tolerances of only inches and no absolute certainty of what lies within:

> *You dash roaring into the small black hole of a tunnel (the impression you get is that it's a marvel you don't miss it sometimes) and when you're in you can see nothing at all. Does that make you slow up? Not at all – not by half a mile per hour. … You can see nothing but the signals – you know your whereabouts simply by memory. … It seemed to me that they went more by the absence of a red light than by the presence of a green one.*
> Eric Gill, *Letters*, ed. Walter Shrewing (1947)

Eurostar trains are more technically advanced than the Gresley 4-6-2s of the era of Gill, but are subject to the same challenges. The Channel Tunnel itself, for example, has piston-relief ducts every 250 metres, creating the occasional 'thwuck' noise heard in transit. Without these, the train would be pushing an intransigent slug of air, not unlike the motion of a bicycle pump. Trains can run through HS1's London and Thames tunnels at speeds of up to 230 kilometres per hour with air-pressure changes limited to a comfortable level. In the much larger double-track North Downs Tunnel, trains can safely pass at up to 300 kilometres per hour without causing the passengers aural discomfort. In the twenty-first century the new tunnels of HS1 are brightly illuminated, clean, sheer and immaculate.

Tunnelling the Thames

Subterranean tunnels have been known throughout recorded history, but submarine tunnels are technically much more difficult, and the River Thames has presented interesting challenges to enterprising engineers since the Dutchman Peter Morris built his waterworks in one of the arches of London Bridge in 1582 to supply houses 'as far as [the very close-by] Gracechurch Street'. Though just 330 kilometres long from its source at Trewsbury Mead, near Cirencester, but passing a great deal of

Marc Brunel's pedestrian Thames Tunnel opened in 1843: a 400-metre-long arched corridor that became known as Hades Hotel.

English history on its way, the great river is a substantial obstacle to be negotiated, both poetically and practically. Yet London Underground travellers are now so familiar with the city's many deep submarine tunnels that the novelty is hard to grasp. The first attempt at any sort of underwater tunnel was by Richard Dodd, in 1799. He began a tunnel under the Thames between Gravesend, Kent, and Tilbury, Essex, but it failed. In 1802 the Thames Archway Company started work on a tunnel from Rotherhithe to Limehouse in east London, resulting initially in a good deal of aimless, uncomfortable fumbling in alluvial silt. The great engineer Richard Trevithick was appointed superintendent of this project in 1805. He employed Cornish miners, who were tough workmen but underestimated the difficulty of excavating the treacherous London clay, resulting in roof-falls and flooding. After little more than 300 metres, this Thames tunnel also failed. In 1809 a learned committee considered if an underwater tunnel was even feasible at all.

Only when Marc Isambard Brunel (1769–1849) and his son Isambard Kingdom Brunel (1806–1859) collaborated on the later Thames Tunnel – the only time the pair worked together – were the problems of submarine tunnelling finally solved. Marc Brunel began work in 1825, his son joining him a year later, aged a mere twenty. They were greatly assisted by the elder Brunel's invention of a tunnel shield, which he patented in 1818. It had been inspired by the shell of the shipworm – a marine mollusc with a natural boring mechanism – that he had observed in 1816 while working at the Naval Dockyards in Chatham, Kent. Carolus Linnaeus, the Swedish botanist, classified the shipworm as 'Teredo navalis or Calamitas navium' (literally 'ship's calamity') on account of its destructive nature. While shipworms had to be kept out of wooden naval vessels, they were nevertheless an inspiration to ambitious engineers.

But the engineer improved on Nature. Brunel's tunnel shield consisted of a huge ring of iron that penetrated the ground, providing not only stability for the structure but also a degree of protection for the workmen, who were normally

TUNNEL-BORING MACHINES

The three types of computer-controlled tunnel-boring machines (TBMs) used on the London Tunnels were manufactured by Wirth, Kawasaki and Lovat, with cutting tools of specially hardened steel. In the autumn of 2002, twin Kawasaki TBMs named 'Annie' and 'Bertha' worked in parallel, boring from Stratford to Gifford Street, near King's Cross. Before work started there was an inaugural libation to Yamano Kami, the Goddess of the Ground, which involved cracking open a wooden barrel of vintage sake. Annie broke through the King's Cross portal on 27 January 2004. The Wirth TBMs were, meanwhile, launched on their 4.7-kilometre journey east from Stratford. These machines were called 'Brunel' and 'Hudson'. The Lovat TBMs, 'Maysam' and 'Judy', excavated the extreme easterly 5.3-kilometre section, from Dagenham.

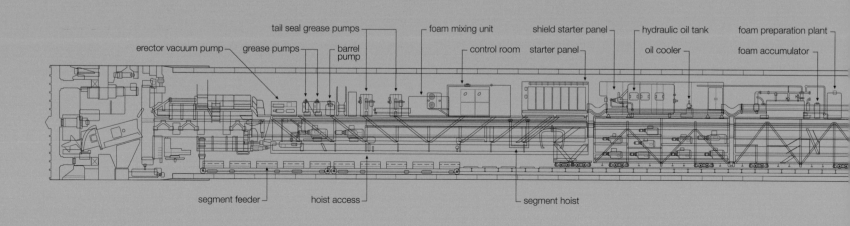

Opposite The world of tunnel digging is not a notably feminine one, but there is a tradition of attributing women's names to the brute TBMs. This is the commissioning of 'Annie' at Kawasaki Heavy Industries, Stockton-on-Tees.

Left 'Annie' is craned into her future workplace in the Stratford Box.

Below A longitudinal section of the tunnel reveals a sophisticated technological process, not a mere dig.

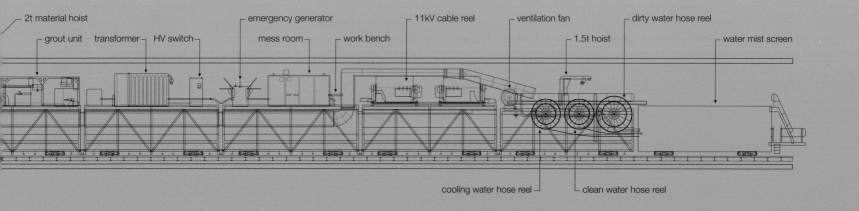

2t material hoist

grout unit   transformer   HV switch

emergency generator

mess room   work bench

11kV cable reel

ventilation fan

1.5t hoist

dirty water hose reel

water mist screen

cooling water hose reel   clean water hose reel

Brunel designed his own TBM and tunnel shield, inspired by a marine mollusc. Work was dangerous and daunting: the excavations were flooded in 1827 and 1828.

at peril in what is quite literally a fluid environment. It was also a dirty, noisy and dangerous one. It is chastening to imagine the noise and the heat, not to mention the darkness, as illumination was by flares only. The iron ring was made by Maudslay Sons & Field of Lambeth, as were the steam pumps that exhausted surplus muddy water, making the venture viable.

Unsurprisingly, progress on the Brunels' Thames Tunnel was slow, perhaps 4 metres a week, and there was flooding in 1827 and again in 1828. After the first flood, which was caused by a roof-fall, Isambard Kingdom Brunel descended in a diving bell to make good the troublesome leak. During the descent, he almost drowned. The project stalled, only to be revived when Marc Brunel secured a £247,000 loan from the Treasury. To help the financial situation, visitors could pay to see the tunnel shield at work. The horrible conditions continued. There was fire-damp (pockets of methane and other gases) and workers suffered from inflammation of the eyes, eruptions of the skin and paralysing fatigue. Brunel noted in his diary: 'Works have been uneasy during the night … ground very tender … ground very threatening … things had a terrific appearance this morning, after a very serious struggle for the night. Illness, the men complain very much … the effluvia was so offensive that some were sick on the stage.'

The Brunels' 400-metre-long arched corridor – the world's first submarine tunnel – opened in 1843 after massive cost over-runs. A Tunnel Waltz was written for the occasion by the Viennese composer Joseph Labitzky, and in fifteen weeks one million curious visitors passed through this Underworld created by modern engineering. It was soon inhabited by a demi-monde whose habits and circumstances suited the foul environment: stallholders selling trinkets were quickly joined by resident prostitutes. They agreed to call it Hades Hotel. The American novelist Nathaniel Hawthorne, writing in 1855, described the 'multifarious trumpery' to be found below, the hookers and thieves operating in the hissy, dank gloom of the submerged gasoliers. Originally intended for horses and carriages, the tunnel was for pedestrians only with access by vertical shafts, owing to a lack of funds to make the necessary

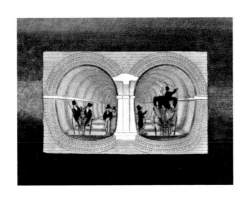

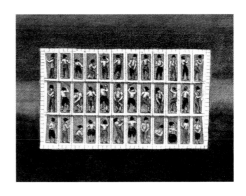

ramps. Still, the American traveller William Allen Drew called it the 'eighth wonder of the world' in his book *Glimpses and Gatherings During a Voyage and Visit to London and the Great Exhibition* of 1851. The reality was perhaps less positive. Indeed, the painter John Martin used promotional illustrations of the Brunel tunnel as inspiration for his popular and terrifying illustration *At the Brink of Chaos* from an edition of John Milton's *Paradise Lost* in 1827. In 1869 the tunnel was converted to rail, the prostitutes and thieves forced to relocate by technological progress. The East London Railway, which ran services through it, became the Southern Railway in 1923. It was amalgamated into London Underground in 1948 and carried the East London line until 2007; it is now part of the London Overground.

Tunnelling HS1

The tunnels along the HS1 track were created by a skilled human workforce, but not the sort of manual labourers known to Brunel. Instead, they were engineers sitting at computer consoles on the vast TBMs (tunnel-boring machines). These adapt Brunel's invention to modern technology, but in essentials are operationally similar. A huge rotating cutting wheel excavating the rock lies at the front of a steel tube. Every 2 metres or so, new rings of pre-cast concrete are put in place. At the rear, hydraulic jacks support the finished parts of the tunnel. Eight specially designed TBMs were used on the major underground sections of HS1: the London and Thames tunnels. But before any tunnelling could even be contemplated, the design of the tunnels and the safe passage of the high-speed trains through their confined spaces had to be determined and proven to satisfy the requirements of the UK safety authorities. Nowhere in the world had such long tunnels been constructed deep under a capital city for trains running at such high speeds. The Channel Tunnel may be longer, but trains are restricted to 160 kilometres per hour and the vibrations generated by the passage of trains

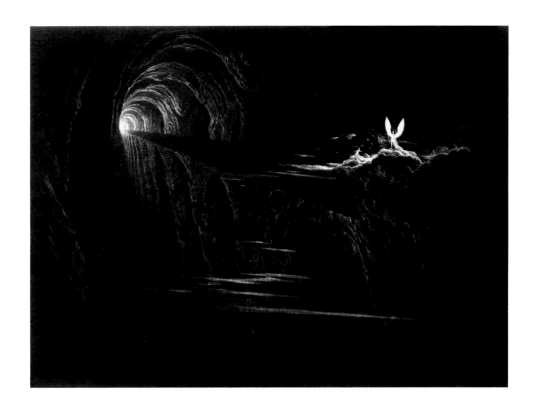

only disturb the fish. The London Tunnels of HS1 contain a sophisticated array of safety measures to deal with a range of potential failures or incidents. The tunnels are equipped with ventilation systems and passenger evacuation walkways joining cross-passages, so that passengers can quickly be moved to safety. A specially designed track-support system incorporating layers of a resilient artificial-rubber material provides a smooth ride for the passenger and a quiet environment for the many residential properties under which the trains pass.

The options for HS1's crossing of the Thames were narrowed down to either a submerged tunnel set into the riverbed or a bored tunnel. The former was resisted by the Port of London Authority, which, understandably, thought a submerged tunnel might be a hazard to vessels navigating the river. At the chosen crossing point, between Swanscombe and West Thurrock, the Thames is not a bucolic river but a busy industrial estuary.

The new Thames Tunnel is 2.5 kilometres of twin single-track bores. Tunnelling began in August 2002 using Herrenknecht TBMs and was safely completed in October 2003, fifty days ahead of schedule. The tunnel incorporates 33,000 concrete ring segments and resulted in 280,000 cubic metres of spoil. At its deepest the tunnel is 45 metres below the surface of the river at high tide. It took Brunel eighteen years to complete the first Thames Tunnel; HS1's tunnel bores were driven in six months for the first and five for the second. These tunnel bores represented the highest construction risk of HS1. High water pressure and fractured chalk containing razor-sharp flint bands were obvious risks, but reliable technology and failsafe systems led to completion on time and without incident.

Viaducts

Calculations about the exact route of the Thames Tunnel had to balance the need to go as deep as possible, to pass safely under the riverbed, with the need to clear the approaches to the Dartford Tunnel Crossing of the M25 motorway. To achieve this, HS1 performs one of its startling feats of improvisatory civil engineering of real genius, the Thurrock Viaduct. *Railway Magazine* called it 'one of the most remarkable pieces of infrastructure on the whole route'. The track becomes airborne to slip over the top of the Dartford Tunnel exit ramps and under the soffit of the QEII Bridge on a 1-kilometre-long viaduct, giving passengers superb westerly views of the Thames estuary. The concrete viaduct was constructed from a launch pad at the London end. Every two weeks a new span was concreted and launched forward, until the final span had been put in place. The entire viaduct, now at its full length of 1025 metres, was then pushed into position and set on its bearings, one year after work on it began. The whole construction was safely carried out without disruption to road traffic on Britain's busiest motorway, the M25.

Crossing under the QEII Bridge was an audacious and highly visible solution to a complex problem, but the run into London was no less of a challenge because of the lush – and sodden – inner Thames marshes. High-speed trains need a firm, secure foundation on which to run, and a wobbly marsh will not do. Making a 7-kilometre crossing of a bog consisting of deep-river alluvium and peat was a Herculean task, solved by the construction of a concrete viaduct supported by piles driven into the underlying chalk. Surprisingly, there is no visible evidence of this structure, as it was constructed at ground level and only rises to pass over existing road or railway crossings.

The easterly approach to London called for the new railway to slice through the industrial land along the side of the Thames, including that belonging to the Ford Motor Company. Here, the problems of disruption to these businesses and the necessary diversion of major pipes and services meant that railway engineers found themselves fulfilling the roles of hard-nosed negotiators and even gas, water and electricity providers.

Below The 1025-metre-long Thurrock Viaduct was built without disruption to the neighbouring M25.

Bottom and opposite
A section of the Thurrock Viaduct: it was built in fortnightly, concreted increments, from a launch pad at the London end.

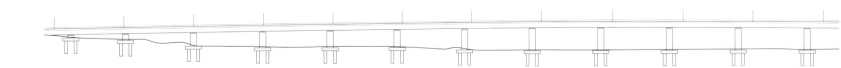

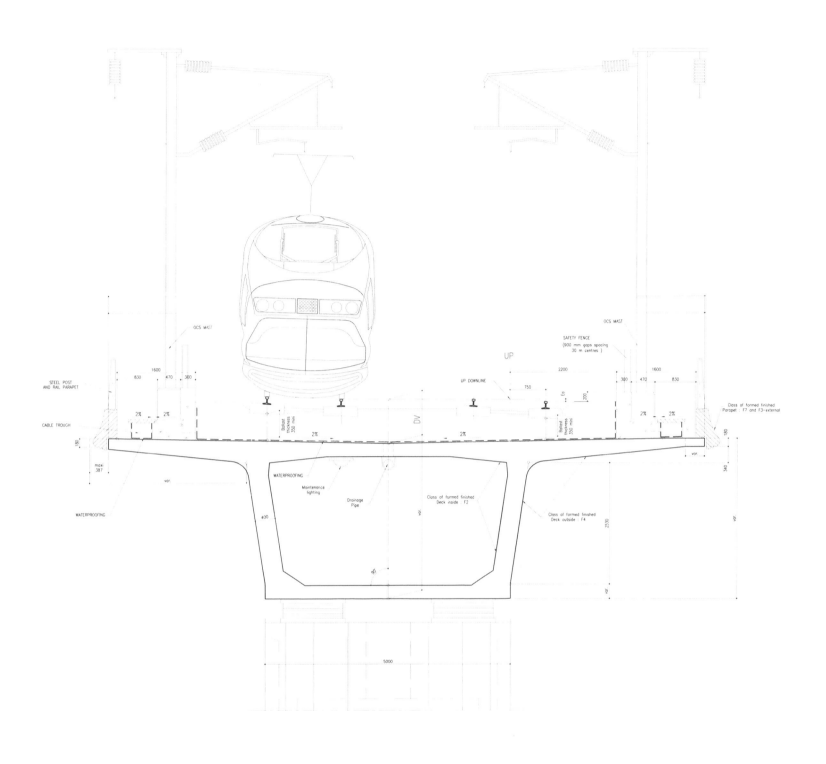

STEEL POST
AND RAIL PARAPET

OCS MAST

OCS MAST

SAFETY FENCE
(900 mm gaps spacing
30 m centres)

UP

UP DOWNLINE

CABLE TROUGH

Class of formed finished
Parapet : F7 and F3-external

1600

830   470   300

2200

750

1600

300   470   830

maxi
387

WATERPROOFING

WATERPROOFING

Maintenance
lighting

Drainage
Pipe

Class of formed finished
Deck inside : F2

Class of formed finished
Deck outside : F4

Ballast
thickness
350 mm

Ballast
thickness
350 mm

2%   2%

2%

2%

2%   2%

180

340

400

2530

var

5000

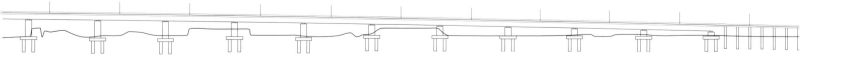

Pages 104–105 High Speed 1 rushes beneath the QEII Bridge and over the approach to the Dartford Tunnel.

Below The approach to Stratford, where the London Tunnel breaks into the light.

The London Tunnels

It was not known what precautions were necessary to ensure the safety of valuable buildings near to the excavations; how to timber the cuttings securely and keep them clear of water without drawing the sand from under the foundations of adjoining houses and within a few inches of the kitchen floors without pulling down anything; how to drive tunnels, divert sewers over or under the railways, keep up the numerous gas and water mains, and maintain the road traffic when the railway is being carried underneath …

Sir Benjamin Baker, Underground pioneer, *c.* 1860

Below The Stratford box:
a concrete masterpiece
more than 1 kilometre long
and 50 metres wide.

Pages 108–109 The
Stratford box after
structural completion, but
before the track was laid.

Pages 110–11 Stratford
International: London's
Olympic station.

The twin-bore London Tunnel, 17.5 kilometres long, below a vast and complex city, presented an exercise in geometry, ingenuity and daring. It is more than three times as long as the Jubilee Line Extension of the London Underground, and was effectively bored as two separate tunnels. It passes beneath 2600 properties, industrial facilities, 67 bridges, 50 masonry retaining walls, 12 kilometres of surface railway, 12 existing tunnels and 600 gas mains, sewers and other vital conduits. At one point near Stratford, the London Tunnel passes within 4.3 metres of the Underground. Shown a true representation of the subterranean complexities, one startled observer said, 'It's spaghetti down there!' Safety considerations led to the splitting of the London Tunnel into two parts, with Stratford at the notional centre, so that emergency crews can access all parts within stipulated time limits.

The London Tunnel goes underground at Ripple Lane, near the Ford manufacturing plant in Dagenham, Essex. There the Lovat TBMs 'Maysam' and 'Judy' drove their way 5.3 kilometres to a midpoint at Barrington Road, Barking, where they met the Wirth TBMs 'Brunel' and 'Hudson', which had excavated the 4.7 kilometres from Stratford (see page 92). The four machines were then dismantled and lifted out of the tunnels through ventilation shafts dug from the surface.

The tunnels emerge into daylight at Stratford, where they pass through a massive open box more than 1 kilometre long and 50 metres wide. This box, big enough to hold three Queen Mary II ocean liners end-to-end, was built by Skanska to contain the new Stratford International station and the junctions necessary to allow trains to pass through at high speed or stop at the platforms. Cross-overs are also provided, so that trains can use either tunnel in the event of delays or problems with rolling stock. A viaduct ramp allows trains from St Pancras to rise 20 metres to ground level to gain access to Eurostar's new

Below, left Advanced concrete construction techniques allow a precision and cleanliness in tunnel building unknown in the past. This is Notting Hill Underground station being built in 1957.

Below, right The old Underground (this is a photograph from 1912) was 'buried beyond the reach of light or life'.

Opposite Sleepers in the London Tunnel are set in concrete, not in crushed stone ballast.

train-maintenance depot at Temple Mills (see pages 128–33). After Stratford, Eurostars shoot underground again, then emerge into the city light to begin a majestic final approach to St Pancras, about a kilometre away to the south.

A photograph of the new London Tunnel makes an astonishing contrast with descriptions in *The Times* and elsewhere of the first Underground tunnels of the mid-nineteenth century as 'buried beyond the reach of light or life'. They were populated by rats, filled with gas that escaped from cracked mains, dampened by London's foul subsoil and leaked foetid water in apocalyptic darkness, with suffocating sulphurous fumes and that strange smell of 'hot' electricity to boot. In the immaculate new tunnels of HS1, the tightness of fit between the ring panels is seeming evidence of the thrilling precision of modern infrastructure, the triumph of technology over natural subterranean impediments. Long before a Eurostar train passed through, the new London and Thames tunnels seemed to invite streamlined vehicles to slither through at very high speeds. Anything less sleek and rapid than Eurostar would be incongruous in such a technically exquisite environment.

The London Tunnel was executed under three separate contracts: the 7.5-kilometre line from Stratford to St Pancras by a joint venture of Nishimatsu, Cementation and Skanska; the 4.7 kilometres from Stratford to the Barrington Road ventilation shaft by a joint venture of Costain, Skanska and Bachy; and the 5.3-kilometre section from Barrington Road to Dagenham by the Edmund Nuttall/ Wayss & Freytag/Kier consortium. This most complex and risky undertaking was completed early and under-budget through a mixture of constructive competition and extraordinary camaraderie between the tunnelling teams.

Along the way, engineers found some of the most testing geology imaginable for tunnelling operations: stiff London clay, shifting sands and gravels, Thanet sand, upper chalk, Thames river terrace gravels, alluvium and peat (see pages 114–15). Without specially developed TBMs, such conditions would have been extremely difficult to cope with. The loose sand was nastily complemented by high water pressure: for much of the route, the water table was close to ground level, so tunnelling was done at up to 3.3-bar water pressure. The Thanet sands, in particular, presented a serious challenge, but with information gained from the construction of the Jubilee line tunnels the engineers knew what to expect. In order to work safely in this difficult environment it was decided to lower the groundwater

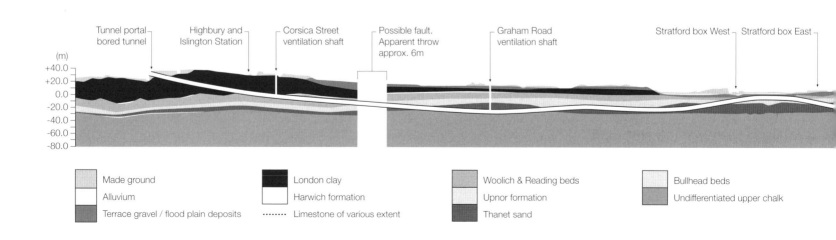

Tunnel portal bored tunnel	Highbury and Islington Station	Corsica Street ventilation shaft	Possible fault. Apparent throw approx. 6m	Graham Road ventilation shaft	Stratford box West	Stratford box East

(m)
+40.0
+20.0
0.0
-20.0
-40.0
-60.0
-80.0

Made ground	London clay	Woolich & Reading beds	Bullhead beds
Alluvium	Harwich formation	Upnor formation	Undifferentiated upper chalk
Terrace gravel / flood plain deposits	········· Limestone of various extent	Thanet sand	

Opposite A TBM breaks through beneath London. 'Overcut', where the bored hole is bigger than strictly necessary, allows the TBM to be steered.

Below Cross-section of the London Tunnel.

Pages 116–17 A bridge carries High Speed 1 over the old East Coast mainline, approaching St Pancras station.

level to below that of the tunnel. 'Dewatering' the ground is a common solution to make work safer and easier for engineers, but these tunnels were 25 metres deep and ran for 12 kilometres through the waterlogged sand. The groundwater level was lowered by drilling a series of deep wells into the chalk along the route, below the level of the Thanet sand, and pumping out the water. (Because this had never been attempted before to such an extent, it took some time to convince all the relevant authorities that parts of London would not sink when the water was extracted.) To give the job a commercial life beyond the requirements of HS1, the system used was designed to Thames Water's specification for abstraction wells and the water sold to the company to supply Londoners.

To ensure that the project was finished on time and within cost, RLE developed a high-performance minimum specification for the bespoke TBMs. All key aspects of the machine were specified, including special high-wear resistant cutter heads, oversize screw conveyor belts, thrust rams, gearboxes and pumps. Long conveyor belts removed spoil continuously; it was transported for reuse to the old Stratford railway lands, which were raised by 7 metres to become a plateau for the Stratford City development (see pages 118–19). The weight of the spoil was analysed constantly, with laser scanners cross-checking volumes. Data was fed both to the TBM operators and to the surface control room throughout the process to highlight any anomalies.

'Overcut', or making a hole bigger than strictly necessary, allows the TBM to be steered and prevents it from getting stuck. As the TBM moved forward, grouting was immediately applied to compensate for any excessive overcut. The 'dewatered' Thanet sand proved very aggressive and resistant to tunnelling, with some of the TBMs running at 110 per cent of their planned maximum torque, generating intense heat: occasionally, sand vitrified on the cutting tools. To reduce the effort required of the machines, water and foam were injected into the cutter head to liquefy the excavated material. Maximum progress was 57 metres a day.

The tunnelling sophistications en route were extraordinary. When work took place near the Central line of the London Underground, the cast-iron rings that comprise tunnels on this part of the network were slightly loosened, to accommodate inevitable flexing during the boring of the London Tunnel.

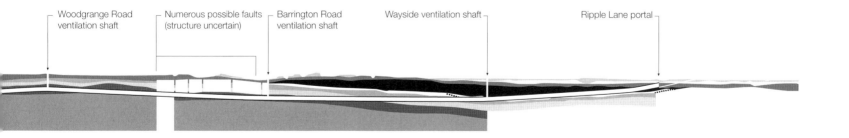

Woodgrange Road ventilation shaft

Numerous possible faults (structure uncertain)

Barrington Road ventilation shaft

Wayside ventilation shaft

Ripple Lane portal

An aerial view of the
Stratford box with Canary
Wharf and the City in the
distance. This will become
the 50-hectare Stratford
City – a major part of the
regeneration excited by
High Speed 1.

Under Caledonian Road the tunnel had to clear a sewer support beam by a mere 0.8 metres, a basement by 3 metres, a large-capacity water main by 4 metres and railway bridge foundations by 4.8 metres. The engineers who built London's first underground railway in the 1850s were continuously beset by cave-ins and the rupture and inundation of the frightful Fleet Ditch sewer. No such emergency occurred with HS1: just one east London garden was lost, surprising its owners, as it descended into the Underworld following tunnelling near what is thought to have been an unmapped well.

The impressive open-cut Stratford box structure, its walls plunging 35 metres into the ground, was excavated with a mixture of hydraulic clamshell grabs and reverse circulation hydromills for the lower, denser strata, and lined with concrete panels up to 1.5 metres thick, cast in-situ. Eighty thousand cubic

metres of soil were excavated from the box and placed, with soil from the tunnel drives, on to the surrounding lands, turning a once-contaminated and low-lying disused railway freight yard into a clean site for a major new development.

That new development is Stratford City, a 50-hectare site roughly the size of Green Park, and the largest mixed-use urban generation project ever to take place in the UK. It was a crucial part of London's successful bid to host the 2012 Olympic and Paralympic Games. The wholesale rejuvenation of Stratford into a vibrant metropolis would have happened with or without the Games, but the prospect of the biggest sporting event in the world gave the development great impetus. The Stratford City masterplan was built on the need for one to benefit the other. The Athletes' Village is structured around 3800 athlete housing units, which will be converted to public housing as soon as the Games finish. HS1 is a thing of rugged beauty, and speed is its very essence, but it is crucial to remember that wealth creation and regeneration are the real reasons for building the high-speed line. Stratford City will provide 34,000 jobs, 5500 homes, 2000 hotel bedrooms, new urban squares, a new city park and 140,000 square metres of shops. In 2009, when domestic high-speed trains will begin using HS1, it will take just seven minutes to get from Stratford to St Pancras International.

'Bridge and tunnel folk' is a term of derision used on Manhattan to stigmatize the provincialism of outsiders, but HS1's bridge and tunnel folk are engineers of distinction with a European perspective. Their model may have been Brunel, not Hart Crane, but there is nevertheless real poetry in the new railway.

Above, left The International Olympic Committee visited Stratford in early 2005. Award of the 2012 Olympics to London followed.

Above, right High-speed rail means you count in minutes, not miles: Stratford International station is 420 seconds from St Pancras.

TRACI
TUNNI
TRAIN
TERMI

'Beyond the throb of the engines is the throbbing heart of all.' John Betjeman

Below The TGV (top) is the technological godparent of Eurostar. Services began between Paris and Strasbourg in 1981. The man who designed its silhouette studied in New York with Raymond Loewy, who designed the GG-1 in 1934 (bottom).

Opposite In or out of a tunnel, above 100 kilometres per hour aerodynamics are critical.

To run a railway you need more than a track: you need trains.

Two types of train are to operate on HS1. The Eurostar is an adaptation of the French *train à grande vitesse* (TGV), which was designed by Alstom and SNCF and entered service in 1981 on the Paris–Lyon route. Before a successful branding exercise of the Channel Tunnel passenger service gave us Eurostar™ (an identity created by the pioneering French designer Roger Tallon) in 1994, the train sets were in fact known as Trans-Manche Super Trains. The TGV is one of the great trains of all time, a machine that changed the perception of travel and its possibilities.

The TGV's distinctive razor-edged snout looks both technical and elegantly feral, as if a sleek beast is sniffing out speed. It was designed by an Englishman, Jack Cooper, who trained in the studio of Raymond Loewy in New York. Loewy was one of the pioneers of consultant design, setting up his own studio in 1927. With a keen perception of the cash value of publicity, Loewy specialized in dramatic shape-making, and his designs often featured in the American illustrated magazines of the 1930s, 1940s and 1950s. His 'GG-1' locomotive for the Pennsylvania Railroad in 1934 became one of the great symbols of streamlined Americana. In its own day this train suggested a future of limitless opportunity for transcontinental travel, 'docile and omnipotent' as Emily Dickinson put it in her poem 'I Like To See It Lap the Miles' (1891). That future never actually arrived for US rail travellers, but it has been a reality in mainland Europe since 1981.

For Eurostar, technical changes to the TGV were necessary because Britain's existing railways have different platform configurations, smaller tunnel and bridge openings, and different power delivery, signalling and communications systems, but it was also felt symbolically important to give a new European train a new European style.

Eurostar's aerodynamics are optimized for high-speed travel. This is not just visual rhetoric: above 100 kilometres per hour in or out of a tunnel aerodynamics become critical for the stability and power consumption of the trains. That distinctive nasal airdam – just like a Formula One car – splits the airflow and helps keep the train stable as it approaches its maximum speed. The distinctive noise of a Eurostar in motion, not dissimilar to the breathy whine of an old Porsche 911, is caused by its enormous cooling fans. (The Porsche sound had the same source.) High-performance vehicles produce heat that needs to be dissipated. A working Eurostar might produce the equivalent of up to 1.3 megawatts of thermal energy from its twelve 1.1-megawatt traction motors. Serious effort is needed to keep the motors cool, especially in tunnels. Hence the whine.

A train depot is a fine place to investigate the sober reality of a Eurostar high-speed train when it is not in service. At 3 kilometres long, and with a 400-metre-long engine and carriage shed containing six tracks, the North Pole

HIGH-SPEED TRAINS: A BRIEF HISTORY

In the 1930s pioneering American
industrial designers, including Raymond
Loewy (1893–1986), Henry Dreyfuss
(1904–1972) and Walter Dorwin Teague
(1883–1960), went to work on
streamlining the US railroads. Loewy's
'GG-1' of 1934 for the Pennsylvania
Railroad and Dreyfuss's '20th Century
Limited' (1) were not technologically
advanced, but presented a stirring visual
rhetoric about the future of rail, its
sophistication, luxury and speed. British
engineers had a more practical attitude
to high-speed aerodynamics: in 1938 Sir
Nigel Gresley's 'A4 Mallard' (3) for LNER
reached 203.6 kilometres per hour, a still-
unbeaten world record for a steam engine.

But by the end of the 1930s steam
power was obsolescent (although it is
estimated that as late as the mid-1970s
about 25,000 steam engines were still
operating throughout the world). Diesels
and electrics, such as General Motors'
'F' series, introduced in 1945, or English
Electric's 1961 'Deltic' (2), paid some
slight attention to styling, but are
essentially fast and efficient, functional
devices. In 1964 Japan launched the
'Shinkansen' (which translates as 'new
main line', after the 515 kilometres of
dedicated new track created for it). It
is universally known as the 'bullet train'
on account of its dramatic form. One
of these trains, the 'Tokaido', was
soon setting records. In 1966 it took
commuters between Tokyo and Osaka
to an unprecedented top speed of
210 kilometres per hour. Bullet trains had
automated signalling, with data passing

directly from rail to driver. The original bullet trains were built by Kawasaki Heavy Industries. The latest generation, the Japan Railways 'Nozomi 500' (4), use Hitachi technology and are styled by German consultant Alexander Neumeister.

In the 1960s maglev (magnetic levitation, where a train is levitated above a steel rail by the attractive and repulsive characteristics of magnets) was still highly experimental, although it has since become a commercial, albeit limited, concern. In pursuit of ever higher speeds, SNCF considered using trains driven by gas turbines, but the oil crisis of 1973 forced a return to conventional electrics. The first TGV reached 300 kilometres per hour in 1981.

Alexander Neumeister designed the exterior of Germany's third-generation high-speed electric train, the 'ICE-3' (5). Some passengers in the front carriage can share the driver's view through sloping forward windows and a glass wall behind the driver. The journey time from Paris to Frankfurt was nearly halved, to 3 hours 49 minutes, when the service was inaugurated in May 2007 (although its introduction was fraught with problems of compatibility between French and German railways). A tilting train, the 'ICE-T', is in development by Siemens.

The current speed record of 574.8 kilometres per hour for a train with conventional wheels was set by a specially adapted TGV running on a closed track on 3 April 2007. Unofficially, Japan's 'JMLX' maglev train has reached 581 kilometres per hour. The fastest regular maglev passenger service is Shanghai's 'Transrapid' airport service, which began in 2004. It can reach 350 kilometres per hour in about two minutes and has a normal operating speed of about 430 kilometres per hour, but travels only along a dedicated 32-kilometre track.

depot in Acton, west London, was the biggest facility of its sort ever to be built in Britain. Here off-duty Eurostars were washed and serviced. When St Pancras replaced Waterloo as the Eurostar terminal, North Pole was itself replaced by a purpose-built Eurostar service facility at Temple Mills, on the site of an old freight depot at Leyton, east London.

The new site is much more efficient: although a little shorter than North Pole (at 2.5 kilometres), it is wider, and its 400-metre-long shed houses eight tracks with lifting gantries, inspection pits and all the necessary equipment needed by highly trained engineers to service the trains' sophisticated equipment. Wheel lathes, toilet discharge facilities and train washers are all strategically arranged at the depot to allow a quick and effective turnaround of the train sets. Lavatories on Eurostars have aircraft-style recirculating systems that in theory can last for a cycle of seventy-two hours before they need emptying. However, prudent servicing means that the discharge operation is usually performed every forty-eight hours. Washing is significant. The reason trains often look dirty in winter is because conventional outdoor train washers, identical (in all except size) to a car wash, are programmed to shut down when the temperature falls below 2°C. At or below this point the water might freeze on to the train body, forming a sheath of ice and effectively 'gluing' the doors shut. The Temple Mills depot is fitted with

This page and opposite; pages 130–31 The Temple Mills site is 2.5 kilometres long, housing eight parallel tracks. Sophisticated maintenance and humdrum toilet discharge take place here.

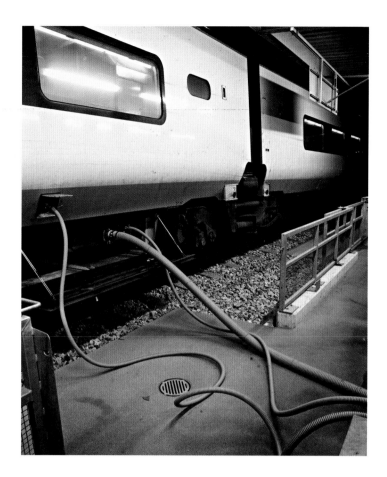

Opposite Temple Mills is designed for rapid turn-around: Eurostars spend very little time standing still.

Above, left The train-washer at Temple Mills can be used in temperatures as low as -2ºC.

Above, right Eurostar uses aircraft-style pressurised plumbing. Toilet discharge takes place every forty-eight hours.

more sophisticated train washers that dry the train before the water has a chance to freeze, and can be used in temperatures as low as -2ºC.

Originally thirty-eight train sets were bought: thirty-one for cross-Channel operations and seven intended for the abortive service to Scotland. A Eurostar 'train set' is a combination of two power cars and eighteen carriages (the North of London train sets have fourteen carriages). Just as the reliability of aircraft is calculated on the basis of 'mean time between failures', that of Eurostar is calculated on the basis of 'incidents per million kilometres'. In this context 'incident' refers to a mechanical or electrical event that prevents the train from reaching its destination within five minutes of its scheduled time. Eurostar aims for not more than twenty incidents per million kilometres: any rate more frequent and more train sets would be needed. And that other reliability question we all yearn to have answered? Well, if one power car unit fails under the Channel, the surviving unit can drag the whole Eurostar on to its destination. Derailing in the tunnel is very unlikely, but, if it happened, the design of the side walls would keep the train upright; it would come to rest after running along the concrete floor. Safety, of course, is crucial, and so the tunnels on HS1 contain evacuation walkways and an impressive range of safety equipment.

Another new element introduced on the TGV and carried over to Eurostar is the placing of bogies between the carriages, a strategy that saves weight by cutting the number of bogies while helpfully improving stability. In the days of steam the driver's cab was at the back of the engine, so the crew could fire the boilers with supplies from the coal wagon, or tender, behind, but the introduction of diesel and electric power changed this arrangement. To avoid distracting reflections in the front screen, the Eurostar cab is strangely dark, although it is not at all like the 'coal-grimed laboratory, the wizard's cell that undertook to contrive

Eurostar interior design by Roger Tallon, France's leading industrial designer, who won the commission in 1987.

The Eurostar driver's cab:
side windows are out of
the driver's field of vision,
avoiding distractions.
The driver must make
an input into a 'vigilance
device' every minute,
otherwise the train brakes
automatically.

a complete transmutation of its surroundings' that Marcel Proust discovered on
his frequent trips. The small side windows are placed out of the driver's field of
vision, so that they too can pose no distraction, even out of the corner of the eye.
The driver sits in the centre of the cabin, surprisingly far back from the single,
small forward screen. Sitting too close to the screen when passing at high speed
through a tunnel can have a mesmerizing effect, lulling drivers into a dangerously
torpid state. Eurostar's dead man's handle, or 'vigilance device', is a foot pedal;
unless the driver uses it to make an input into the system every minute, a human
casualty is inferred and the train brakes automatically. Eurostars are continuously
monitored for speed over the safe limit, and are automatically stopped if they are
found to be travelling unaccountably fast.

Train brakes still use technology essentially derived from American
engineer George Westinghouse's original pneumatic system of 1869. The
mechanism that supplies the compressed air to power the brakes can still be
heard cycling on and off, punctuated by the sound of a pressure-relief valve. On
Eurostar, the powered wheels have tread brakes, where cast-iron blocks halt the
motion of the wheels. The trailer wheels are stopped by means of discs.

The sleek, international Eurostars will share HS1 with domestic high-speed
trains. In December 2009 twenty-nine Hitachi Class 395 bullet trains will take to
the route, providing train company Southeastern's high-speed services for Kent
and south-east England and dramatically changing the geography of a part of the
country that has a real need for speed.

Class 395s are capable of running at up to 225 kilometres per hour. The
trains are aluminium-bodied for lightness and strength, enhanced by friction
stir welding (FSW), which is stronger than conventional metal inert gas (MIG)
welding. This technique, never before used on UK mainline rolling stock, allows

Hitachi Class 395 trains
begin domestic high-speed
services in 2009.

construction to very high tolerances without deformation. Each train has an on-board monitoring and recording device similar to an aircraft's 'black box', constantly logging driver and mechanical inputs. In addition, there is a Train Protection Warning System (TPWS) and an Automatic Warning System (AWS).

The new trains are likely to become embedded in the public psyche when London hosts the Olympic and Paralympic Games in 2012, when the Class 395s will provide a high-speed shuttle service for spectators. For this great sporting event, this international celebration of athletic fraternity and organized tourism, the 'bullet' trains will be tastefully rebranded 'Javelin', and each will be named after a Briton noted for speed, not after politicians or PR men.

Domestic high-speed trains will 'shrink' Kent in terms of the time taken to reach important destinations. No longer will passengers have to chug through the Garden of England, enduring journeys recalling an era when time was less important: in 2009 it will take less than forty minutes to get from London to Ashford. The journey to Canterbury will be halved to sixty-one minutes, and Dover will be little over an hour away, instead of the current hour and fifty-two minutes. East Kent has become part of London.

The Journey

The passenger cabins are lightly pressurized and the experience is insulated from the dramatic reality of high-speed terrestrial travel. The driver is similarly isolated in his cab. The drama described by Eric Gill when, in pursuit of an experience to bring him closer to his idealized concept of the nobility of labour, he stood on the footplate of an old steam express has completely disappeared:

All the luxury and culture of the world depends ultimately upon the efforts of the labourer … . And just as the passenger very seldom thinks about the men on the engine, so we thought nothing at all about the passengers. They were simply part of the load. … the absence of connection between engine and train was emphasized by the entirely different physical sensations which engine travelling gives you. The noise is different – you never for a moment cease to hear, and to feel, the effort of the pistons. The shriek of the whistle splits your ears, a hundred other noises drown any attempt at conversation …

Eric Gill, *Letters*, ed. Walter Shrewing (1947)

The soot, din and danger of early rail travel are also evoked in J.M.W. Turner's romantic homage to the first age of the train, his huge canvas *Rain, Steam and Speed*, now in London's National Gallery. It was painted in 1844 in response to the railway mania then sweeping the country. Within a few years 815 railway ventures had come before Parliament, in an early Victorian version of the dotcom boom and bust of the early twenty-first century. Turner's setting has been confidently identified as the Great Western Railway's Maidenhead Bridge, designed by Isambard Kingdom Brunel and opened in 1839. In front of the steaming train runs a hare, one of the fleetest of animals, at perhaps 50 kilometres per hour. It was safe in front of Turner's steam train. Speed meant something rather different in 1844.

Gill also described the characteristic movement of travelling by steam train: 'Iddy umty … iddy umty … is the rhythmic tune you hear in the train.' That is just one way low-speed rail travel differs from the high-speed option. Rail travel in the past was romantic, but uncomfortable; the new reality is different. No more shuffling gouts of steam. Philip Larkin's London seen from the train was 'spread out in the sun,/ Its postal districts packed like squares of wheat'. Approaching the station he noted 'this frail/ Travelling coincidence; and what it held/ Stood ready to be loosed with all the power/ That being changed can give. We slowed again,/ And as the tightened brakes took hold, there swelled/ A sense of falling, like an arrow shower/ Sent out of sight, somewhere becoming rain.'

Eurostar passengers enjoying high-speed rail travel can feel Larkin's romance, but their overall experience will be different. People used to say it is better to travel than to arrive. Sometimes, but not always. The HS1 terminus at St Pancras tests that old trope.

TRACI
TUNNI
TRAIN
TRACI
TRAIN
TERMI

NUS

'Railway termini … are our gates to the glorious and the unknown. Through them we pass out into adventure and sunshine, to them, alas! we return.'
E.M. Forster, 'Howards End' (1910)

The study of railway stations, according to the poet John Betjeman, is something like the study of churches. He said that where in one you have a piscina (basin), in the other you find a cast-iron lamp bracket. For transepts, read waiting rooms. For altar cloths, advertisements. Now you can add loft apartments, champagne bars, brasseries, high-quality bakeries, farmers' markets and luxury-goods shops. St Pancras is now, in every sense, the ultimate destination station. But its story is as long and involved, comic, tragic and circuitous as the modern railway it represents.

In 1974, in the early days of HS1, it was thought that no existing London mainline station had room for expansion to meet the anticipated volume of passengers for international services. Bizarrely, in retrospect, Clapham Junction and Kensington Olympia were considered as options for development. Long before the new track was laid – in fact, when people actually thought a new track was impossible – another alternative was an interchange at Sellindge in rural Kent (the village where, eventually, Talbot House was moved out of the way of HS1; see page 61). Fast French trains that could penetrate sleepy Albion no further would stop here, and passengers would be transferred to the then decrepit local service.

Later, a report identified fifty-two possible London candidates for the terminus of the high-speed line. In 1989 it was announced that King's Cross in north London would be considered alongside Waterloo in south London. The

Right Waterloo International station, 1993: Eurostar's first London terminus seen from the air.

Opposite, top Waterloo International's site was constricted.

Opposite, bottom Architect Nicholas Grimshaw's technophiliac structure at Waterloo International introduced the first generation of Eurostar passengers to the reality of high-speed rail travel.

former had the benefit of access to Scotland and northern England through the mainlines, as well as suburban Thameslink (now First Capital Connect) and Underground connections. One early concept for the station envisaged an entirely subterranean terminus with eight platforms: six for Eurostar and two for Thameslink.

In the end Waterloo was chosen as Britain's new international terminal for Eurostar in 1987. The new station was a dramatic and elegant design in steel and glass by the architectural practice of Nicholas Grimshaw. The cramped and sinuous site had to be adapted and extended to accommodate Eurostars, which are nearly 400 metres long. Grimshaw's response was to create a bold, arching exoskeleton over a curving vault. His design was interpreted by the engineers Anthony Hunt Associates, who used CAD techniques of structural analysis to help achieve the complex fit and parametric relationships that make Waterloo International such a distinguished piece of architecture, a fine contrast to the original Waterloo, described by John Betjeman as 'mean and ostentatious'. Grimshaw's high-tech structure was completed in May 1993 at a cost of about £130 million. The old St Pancras station was then a striking contrast to this modern jewel.

John O'Connor, *Sunset – St Pancras Hotel and Station from Pentonville Road*, 1881. One of the most romantic paintings of London features the station.

The commission for St Pancras station

St Pancras is a station apart, a Royal station. The old idea that the Midland was the most comfortable railway in the world still holds good. ... I have no doubt that British Railways will do away with St Pancras altogether. It is too beautiful and too romantic to survive. It is not of this age.

John Betjeman, *Flower of Cities* (1949)

'The station distils the very essence of Mid-Victorian power: for it is the most magnificent commercial building of the age, reflecting more completely than any other its economic achievement, its triumphant technology, its assurance and pride, suffused by romance', wrote Jack Simmons, historian of St Pancras, in *St Pancras Station* (1968/2003). St Pancras has been described in many ways. It is a 'Gothic phantasmagoria' and an 'inestimable' contribution to the London skyline, according to David Piper, in his elegant *Companion Guide to London* (1964/2000). To the writer Ian Nairn, in one of his fits of puritanism, it was merely 'fancy work', neither so fine nor so worthy as the sterner King's Cross next door, a more obviously engineered structure (*Nairn's London*, 1966). Sir John Summerson, an architectural historian with a special interest in classicism, found the exuberant Gothic of St Pancras 'nauseating'. It is regularly described as a wall of red brick (in fact, it is built of Gripper's Patent Nottingham stock with dressings in Ancaster stone punctuated by shafts of grey and red Peterhead granite). The romance of St Pancras and that fairytale skyline was captured sentimentally in oils by John O'Connor in his canvas *Sunset – St Pancras Hotel and Station from Pentonville Road* of 1881. More recently, and incongruously, the exterior of St Pancras was used to

represent King's Cross station in two of the Harry Potter films (*Harry Potter and the Sorcerer's Stone* and *Harry Potter and the Chamber of Secrets*).

Along with the Foreign Office and the Albert Memorial, the southern portion of St Pancras is an outstanding monument of Victorian architecture. All three were designed by the same man, Sir George Gilbert Scott (1811–1878). A 'battle of the styles' characterized High Victorian architecture, and in the 1860s Gothic was dominant. It was in this decade that Scott produced five major Gothic buildings: the Foreign Office in Whitehall, London; Glasgow University; Dundee's Albert Institute; the parish church at Kensington, London; and St Pancras. Scott was the most prolific architect of his day, but not always the most admired. 'Only Cardiganshire', someone once said, 'is Scott-free.' His greatest masterpiece of secular Gothic, the Albert Memorial, had recently been controversial, and in 1877 William Morris accused him of 'feeble and lifeless forgery'. Strange, then, that Scott's own conviction was that A.W.N. Pugin's Gothic Revival, which he discovered in his thirties, was the basis of a 'deep-seated, earnest and energetic revolution in the human mind'.

Scott was one of the first Victorians fully to exploit the railways as a commercial enterprise. Rather as today's global celebrity architects exist in a netherworld of airport lounges and first-class in-flight service, so Scott inhabited the world described in Thomas Hardy's poem 'Faintheart in a Railway Train': 'At nine in the morning there passed a church,/ At ten there passed me by the sea,/ At twelve a town of smoke and smirch,/ At two a forest of oak and birch.' There are several stories about Scott and the railways. Once, on a journey, his hard-pressed assistant was asked by Scott, 'Who designed that church?', and the answer was, 'You did, sir.' On another occasion, just as a leading architect today may not know whether he or she is in London, Los Angeles or Paris airports, Scott arrived at a Midlands station and had to telegraph his London office demanding 'Why am I here?'

Above George Gilbert Scott, Albert Memorial (1863–72; top) and Glasgow University (1864–70).

Right George Gilbert Scott, St Pancras station, 1866–73. It was 'too beautiful and too romantic to survive', according to John Betjeman.

Pages 148–49 George Gilbert Scott's original drawing of the façade of 'The Midland Railway Terminus'.

MIDLAND RAILWAY TERMINUS.
St. Pancras Station and Hotel.

No. 10

SAINT PANCRAS

An image of Saint Pancratius in stained glass from the west choir of Naumburg Cathedral in Germany, *c.* 1250. He is now International.

There are two or three obscure saints known as Saint Pancras. The first was a fourteen-year-old boy who defended the Christian faith under the persecution of the Emperor Diocletian. As a consequence, he was stoned and put to the sword in 304 AD. A church of San Pancrazio has existed near the Porta di San Pancrazio in Rome since about 500 AD. Most of this saint's remains are there, although his head is in San Giovanni Laterano. This Saint Pancras is the avenger of false witness and false oaths. His feast day is 12 May.

Another Pancras, or Pancratius, was sent by Saint Peter to preach the gospel to the Sicilians, then much given to the worship of idols. In Taormina, Pancratius threw the local idols, Pholco and Lyssio, into the sea, setting up a redemptive figure of Christ in a tower as a replacement. The heathens objected, and for his trouble Pancratius too was stoned. Taormina's church of San Pancrazio is outside the city's Porta Messina, on the site of a Greek temple. This saint's feast day is 3 April.

The third Saint Pancras, who is sometimes confused with the first, was beheaded in Rome in the fourth century. His remains were brought to England in the seventh century by Pope Vitalian. A church was named after him in Canterbury, Kent.

Above Lewis Cubitt's façade of King's Cross revealed the structure of what lay behind.

Below, left and right The architecture of Scott's St Pancras was determined by a need to be distinguished from the functional austerity of the neighbouring King's Cross.

An early edition of *Bradshaw's Railway Guide* shows that the first railway lines only tentatively approached the centre of London. In 1837 Euston was the first mainline station and, like its immediate contemporaries, the other stations in north-central London, was more connected to the delicacies and refinements of the Georgian era than to the swagger and bluster of High Victoriana. The strangeness of railway stations fascinated Marcel Proust, who thought of them as 'those peculiar places … which scarcely form part of the surrounding town but contain the essence of its personality'. The cluster of new stations, from Euston in the west through to King's Cross and St Pancras in the east, was built on semi-rural land. As late as 1803 William Blake wrote in *Jerusalem* of 'the fields from Islington to Mary[le]bone'. The Metropolitan Railway Commissioners in 1846 actually prevented the railways moving further into the centre of the city.

These great termini were defined by branding, the needs of the pioneer railway companies to express their corporate identity, although it was not at the time so known. Euston was in one style, King's Cross another. The style of the new St Pancras was determined almost in opposition to Lewis Cubitt's austere King's Cross, the façade of which was a clear diagram of what lay behind. At King's Cross the architect was alone satisfied by 'the largeness of some of the features, the fitness of the structure for its purpose, and a characteristic expression of that purpose', at least, according to *The Builder* in 1851. In 1952 Nikolaus Pevsner sniffily said no one would think that about St Pancras.

Shortly after its incorporation in 1844, the ambitious Midland Railway decided it needed a London terminus of its own. So, in 1865 it built its own line from Bedford to a site in the old Agar Town 'rookery' of north London, a notorious slum (where Dan Leno was born in 1861) and an area reputed for its endemic wickedness, want and beggary. Like all London slums of the day, it was a mixture of gin shops and brothels, a network of musty yards and cramped passages, where the buildings were packed so tightly that one had to turn sideways to pass between them. With his reporter's eye, Charles Dickens described the neighbourhood as having 'a profound attraction of repulsion'. He saw 'an English suburban Connemara – a complete bog of mud and filth with deep cart ruts, wretched hovels, the doors blocked up with mud, heaps of ashes, oyster shells and decayed vegetables. The stench … is enough to knock down a bullock.' Into this sordid milieu the mighty Midland proposed to

St Pancras station in 1876. Platforms 3 and 4 were yet to be built; the space between platforms 5 and 2 was used for storing carriages.

put its landmark. Scott was one of eleven leading architects invited to compete for the design of a new station and hotel. In 1866 it was announced that he had won the competition, although at £316,000 his design was the most expensive.

The train shed

Another of the strange and evil tendencies of the present day is to the decoration of the railroad station. … It is the very temple of discomfort, and the only charity that the builder can extend to us is to show us, plainly as may be, how soonest to escape from it. …
John Ruskin, *The Lamp of Beauty* (1889)

But the red-brick landmark is not St Pancras station itself, only a hotel that came a little later to front it. The general arrangement of the station was determined by the fact that the railway, approaching from the north, has to rise over Regent's Canal and therefore arrives at about 6 metres above street level. This was in part a bravura gesture by the Midland Railway, keen to demonstrate engineering expertise and daring, but, more prosaically, it also created an undercroft where the brewer Bass of Burton-on-Trent could store its beer. Indeed, in a paper to the Institution of Civil Engineers in 1870, W.H. Barlow (1812–1902), the engineer who built St Pancras's train shed, noted that 'the length of the beer barrel became the unit of measurement upon which all the arrangements of this floor were based'. Horse urine, rope and tree trunks were allegedly involved in the manufacture of the cast-iron columns; no one quite knows how. The columns brace a grid of 2000 iron girders supporting iron plates, upon which rests the iron track. Scott's original design for the St Pancras hotel was the public face of the no-less-remarkable engine shed behind. In its contrast and combination of otherworldly medieval and mythic excess with raw engineering of great invention and refinement, St Pancras is a doubly evocative monument to Victorian achievement. Barlow had hitherto worked on lighthouses in the Bosphoros and had been ennobled by the Turks, before assisting in the design of the Crystal Palace for the Great Exhibition of 1851 in London and finishing the Clifton Suspension Bridge after Isambard Kingdom Brunel's death in 1859. He was, nonetheless, more self-effacing than the over-energetic Scott.

The Barlow shed is a magnificent tied arch, an iron-and-glass span 74 by 210 metres, a 'vast throbbing hangar' filled with 'overwhelming solid force', according to Ian Nairn. Barlow's aim had been to provide a visually elegant, structurally efficient and economically low-cost structure. Twenty-five arches of riveted iron are placed at centres 8.9 metres apart. They support about 1 hectare of glass, and, of course, their own weight. Barlow's sublime roof actually reaches a point about 32 metres above the rails. It would be idle to suggest that an engineer as committed to rationality as Barlow might have wanted to evoke a Gothic pointed arch in metal. The pointed section was a means of dealing with loads caused by the weight of the roof. Still, he conceded that the result was an 'architectural effect', which meant it had a certain decorative intention. Scott and Barlow certainly had contrasting styles and materials, but their intention was the same: to make St Pancras astonishing.

Above, left Joseph Paxton's Crystal Palace, the world's first major prefabricated glass and iron structure, c. 1850.

Above, right W.H. Barlow, designer of the St Pancras train shed, worked on the Clifton Suspension Bridge after Isambard Kingdom Brunel's death in 1859.

Pages 154–55 St Pancras in 1876, three years after the hotel opened. Hotel guests were protected from noise and dirt by demountable screens.

RESHMENT ROOM

In realizing the shed, Barlow was assisted, to varying degrees, by two remarkable figures. The first was the engineer Rowland Mason Ordish, designer of bridges in Prague, St Petersburg, Singapore and London, where his delightful Albert Bridge in Chelsea opened in 1873. The second was the poet Thomas Hardy, working as an architectural assistant to Arthur Blomfield, whose office was engaged to clear up St Pancras Old Church's graveyard, which stood in the way of metropolitan progress. As the clearances took place, Hardy noted an erupting infernal apocalypse of thigh bones and skulls, soil that he called 'mixed to human jam'. The motif recurred frequently in such poems of his as 'The Levelled Churchyard' and 'In the Cemetery', to such an extent that it is fair to surmise that the whole experience confirmed for him the presence of death in life. He writes, from the corpses' point of view: 'O passenger pray list and catch/ Our sighs and piteous groans.' A thriving 'Hardy Tree' still stands in St Pancras Churchyard, surrounded by a jumble of confused headstones: the dead making way for the travelling.

The Midland Grand Hotel

Barlow's design for the train shed was approved on 3 May 1865, at the same Midland Railway meeting that put the design of the intended new hotel out to the competition eventually won by George Gilbert Scott. For a long time it was thought that Scott's design for the Midland Grand Hotel was merely a warmed-up version of his original proposals for the Foreign Office, grandiosely rejected by Lord Palmerston. The story owes its origin to a passage in Scott's autobiography, where he says the hotel design 'is possibly too good for its purpose', but the truth is that having studied so much French and Italian Gothic detail, he simply wanted it put to good use.

The result looks like nothing English nor anything truly medieval. In fact, it looks like what it was: an original of 1866. The Midland Grand Hotel opened on 5 May 1873 at a cost of £438,000. Its manager was one Robert Etzensberger, who had worked in the Venetian hotel trade and was thus aware of advanced consumer tastes. The entrance had a fabulously elaborate double staircase, a Turkish kiosk serving coffee, Arthurian wallpaper and one of London's first hydraulic 'ascending rooms', that is, a lift. This last was a great novelty, installed only in the other great London hotels of the day: the Charing Cross, the Grosvenor, the Westminster Palace and the Langham. But, to complement the lift, the Midland Grand retained a ceremonial staircase of girders, treads and brackets rising through three floors of the building. While in his Albert Memorial Scott hid the structural ironwork behind the decorative effects, here – while there are voluptuous crimson-and-gold fleurs-de-lis – horizontal metal beams are daringly, if incongruously, expressed. For Scott, the 'feeble forger', this was impressively explicit structural detail. When lifts eventually became commonplace, the ceremonial staircase fell out of use, surviving only to connect the lobby with the first floor.

Facilities in the Midland Grand included a Coffee Room, featuring polished stonework decorations with foliate themes of vine, fern and pomegranate. Further dedicated rooms were given over to smoking, billiards and hairdressing. A Ladies' Coffee and Dining Room was on the first floor. An 'Electrophone', a contraption distantly related to the telephone, allowed ladies, some of them smoking, to listen to concerts below. As Simon Bradley has noted in his superlative book on St Pancras station (2007), 'To imagine a fashionable lady of 1900 in this room, straining to decode the muffled chords of Wagner or Debussy above the roar of horseshoes and cartwheels, is to feel the poignancy of the gulf between the present and the not so distant past.' Only nine bathrooms were provided at first, portable commodes and hip baths allowing for the vital ablutions that only much later became a plumbed-in assumption of hotel life.

Above The Midland Grand's fabulous double staircase in a gorgeous High Victorian interior.

Left The Midland Grand's first-floor music room (far left) and its dining-room.

Ian Nairn called the whole design 'incredibly clever … and incredibly heartless'. The classicist Summerson saw the dichotomy between Barlow's 'noble' shed and Scott's 'gingerbread' as melancholy proof of a ruinous professional schism emerging in the later nineteenth century between engineer and architect. Art historian Hilary Spurling said Scott's 'aim was to ransack the past, invoke the future and dominate the present'. Both engine shed and station hotel were soon subject to small modifications. Barlow had painted his ironwork brown, but it was changed to sky blue. The Midland Grand received, from New York, London's first revolving door, but this innovation was not enough to prevent the hotel shutting down in 1935, hopelessly old-fashioned, and beginning a journey of neglect and decay. So, far from realizing Scott's anticipated 'energetic revolution in the human mind', St Pancras became an indictment and an embarrassment.

The derelict Midland Grand attracted movie-makers and photographers, including the Californian Richard Ross, who took this picture in 2002.

Barlow's shed fared better, but was pitiably underused and poorly maintained. At one point, corrugated iron was used to patch damaged glazing in the magnificent vault. The old British Rail had been determined to demolish St Pancras, even after it was listed as being of Grade I historic importance in 1967 (chiefly through the intervention of John Betjeman). As there was no money to spend on rolling stock, let alone architecture, the fabric of a Victorian masterpiece was simply allowed to rot. Grudging, makeshift, clumsily improvised attempts at stabilization – including pouring concrete around rusting iron 'boots' in the underground vault that supports the great engine shed – only made the ultimate restoration more difficult. In order to appreciate the achievement of the past few years, the creation of HS1 and the thrilling and meticulous restoration of a much-loved London landmark, it is only necessary to recall how, until very recently, St Pancras and its environs were desolate and bereft, put almost beyond use by neglect, philistinism and incompetence.

Travelling down Pentonville Road on an evening with a good sunset, north Londoners were, as they had been for 150 years, treated to one of the most evocative sights in the capital: the craggy, spiky skyline of the station hotel. Not, perhaps, as swaggering as Mad King Ludwig's Schloss Neuschwanstein, a saccharine, theatrical confection of turrets and crenellations in the Bavarian Alps, but instead a practical monument to Victorian business. Long before Hogwarts introduced a Gothick sensibility to popular culture, the prolific George Gilbert Scott had done so on behalf of the Midland Railway. This was architecture in the service of corporate identity, before the kerbflash of mirrored glass and atriums. But by 2002 the old Midland Grand Hotel, the railway that supported it and St Pancras station itself had gone the way of Empire, which is to say not down the tracks, but down the tube. When the hotel closed in 1935 the St Pancras area began to return to the condition in which Dickens had found it in 1851.

Although in 1977 St Pancras was saved from the siren-call of predatory developers by a Victorian Society campaign led by John Betjeman and Nikolaus Pevsner, it had been in physical decline ever since: no bullocks were left standing along the Euston Road. The transition to corruption was memorably recorded by the Getty Museum photographer Richard Ross in 2002. He found film and television crews had been working there and explained, 'I haunt old places … they allowed me to explore the depths of the place … you have the real nostalgia of the building mixed with the remnants of a Johnny Depp movie and Harry Potter … seeming like a teenage angst-ridden room.' Certainly, Ross's pictures describe a sort of Herculaneum of hotel horror: peeling wallpaper, corrupt modern nylon carpet abutting a fine marble fire surround, safety lights and fluorescent tubes insolently in front of Gothick mullions, a stacking chair in front of grimy frosted glass and lavatory stalls furnished with plastic seats that Scott would not have squatted on. Ross said of St Pancras, 'There is no reality there any more.' But by 2007, that had all changed.

The restoration of St Pancras

Now St Pancras is something rather different. Officially, it is Area 100 of Section 2, undertaken by the contractor CORBER (Costain, Laing O'Rourke, Bachy Soletanche and Emcor), an £800 million part of this £5.8 billion project. Now its painstaking, splendid refurbishment and development are the visible symbol of Europe's most ambitious civil-engineering project. The new railway is impressive in itself – 110 kilometres of fast track, a quarter of it underground, plus 150 bridges and viaducts – and the ultimate realization of the dreams of the Victorian railway pioneers. So it is wonderfully appropriate that the terminus of this realized dream is another expression of Victorian genius: a monumental urban presence

BURTON BEER: THE MEASURE OF ST PANCRAS

Burton-on-Trent, Staffordshire, was the most famous brewing centre in the UK. Its beers were already well-known in London in the seventeenth century. This East Midlands town enjoys exceptionally high-quality fresh water because of the high local levels of gypsum. In a system known as the 'Burton Unions' (but also used in other towns) yeast was cultivated and 'exercised' through a linked system of beer barrels to give a distinctive taste. The old brewers of Burton popularized pale ale in the nineteenth century, as the railways made it easier to distribute branded goods nationwide. Chief among the brewers was Bass, which produces a beer with a specific gravity of 1044 kilograms per cubic metre, regarded by connoisseurs as the definitive pale ale. The international beer expert Michael Jackson says Bass has a 'distinctive fruitiness' but is 'slightly sour', giving it a 'unique character, irresistible to its admirers'. Bass is now owned by the US Molson-Coors conglomerate. The yeast extract Marmite, a by-product of the processes involved in making beer, is also manufactured in Burton.

now rededicated to all the social and economic possibilities of fast, seamless, modern travel. W.H. Barlow's soaring glass vault and George Gilbert Scott's evocations of the crockets and towers of Verona and Flanders, of Amiens, Caen and Venice – a Victorian maestro would make free with his sources – are not gone, but have been brightened and tightened after years of dismaying neglect.

Building a new box under King's Cross had been considered while the route was still planned to approach it from the south, via Waterloo, but once the high-speed route through Stratford had been decided, the opportunity to realize the neglected potential of St Pancras appeared as if in a revelation. Clearly, an existing landmark building was an advantage in any plan to make the new St Pancras a destination in itself, but vast and daunting infrastructural changes were required before that pleasant attribute could be enjoyed. For example, the idea of exploiting the undercroft for the benefit of international travellers could only come to fruition once the existing tracks of the Midland Mainline railway had been repositioned. This was done without interruption to service by moving the railway lines first one way and then another to make space for the works. Four new platforms were constructed on the east deck extension, and the trains moved out of the original train shed. Two more platforms were then added alongside to accommodate the Thameslink trains while the tunnel under St Pancras was demolished and a new underground station created for the Thameslink. With the Thameslink trains returned to their underground route, work could start on the western deck extension. Once it was finished Midland Mainline trains could occupy their new platforms and the work on the track leading to the international platforms could be completed. This movement of tracks and platforms was made all the more complicated by the fact that road traffic around and under the station had to be maintained and old pipes and services (including the Fleet Sewer and major gas-distribution mains) diverted.

Although the old cast-iron columns were found to be sound, Barlow's deck of horizontal wrought-iron ties was supplemented – in one of the most radical architectural alterations made to the station – by a new concrete slab floor, pierced to illuminate the lower levels and, more prosaically, allow escalator access. What had once held firkins of Bass beer became an international arrivals and departures hall. (Workmen drilling out the old iron deck were suspended in safety harnesses as a precaution against the sudden collapse of the old floor.) On top of the remaining cast-iron columns (587 of the original 691) there is now a sandwich of high-specification grout, setting in place new bearings, which allow lateral movement of the concrete deck. While the cast-iron columns are immensely strong in compression, they are vulnerable to lateral loads. The combination of the dynamic loads of the trains and the thermal loads of heating will cause the concrete deck to move, and the bearings allow it to do so without exposing the historic columns to destructive forces. International passengers eating brioches in this undercroft are brushing past a meticulous restoration of Victorian ingenuity.

The shed ironwork was grit-blasted and reglazed to Barlow's original specification, after a survey by intrepid abseilers. Inside, seven tower cranes and 1000 men worked with cherry-pickers among temporary scaffolding. Pick-up trucks ran up and down the train trackbeds. By May 2005 Barlow's restored shed, its ridge-and-furrow design reinstated after bomb damage and years of neglect, was beginning to emerge from its chrysalis of construction plant.

The design of the new St Pancras is the work of RLE, working to an initial masterplan devised by Norman Foster. RLE developed the plan for the restoration of the listed train shed under the direction of its lead architect, Alastair Lansley, and technical director, Mike Glover, both of Arup. Not only have Scott's Gothic brickwork and Barlow's ironwork been restored, but also a brand-new

WORK / TERMINUS

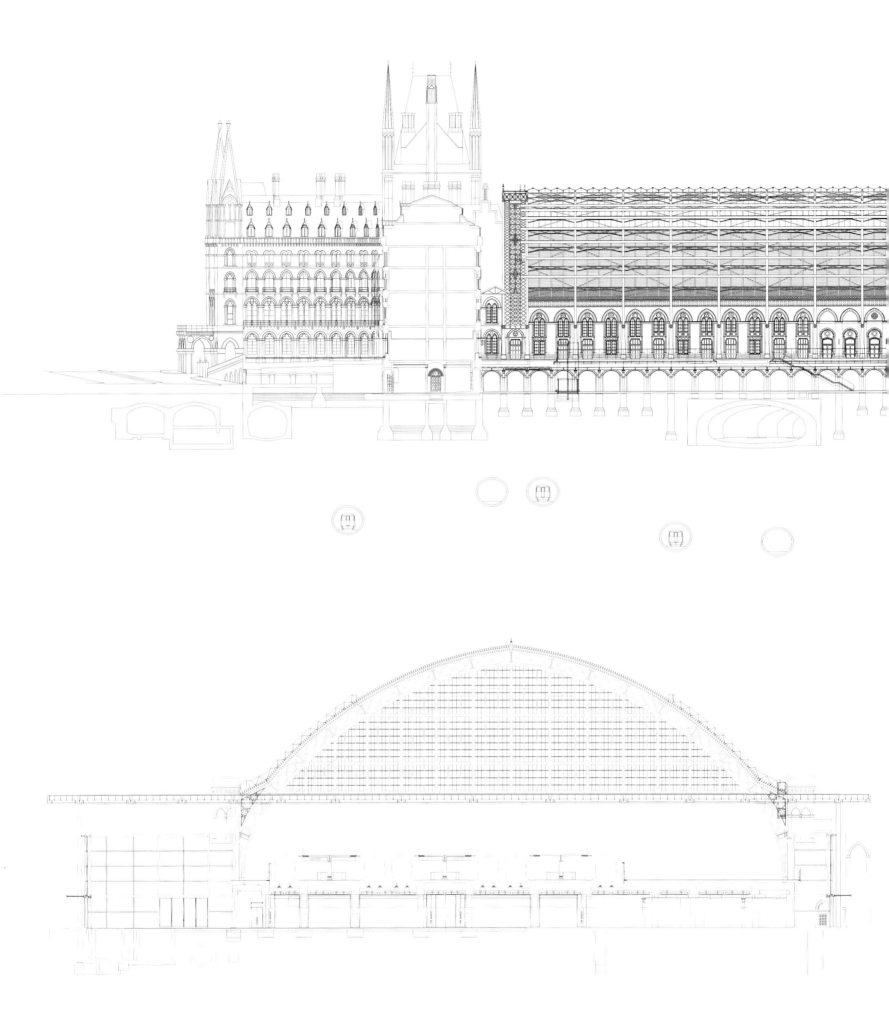

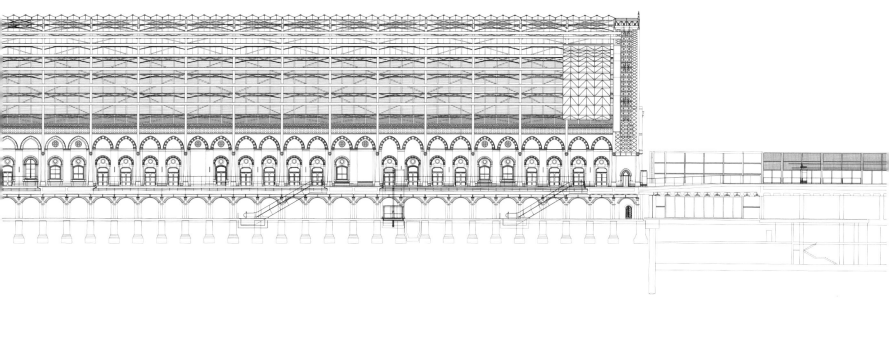

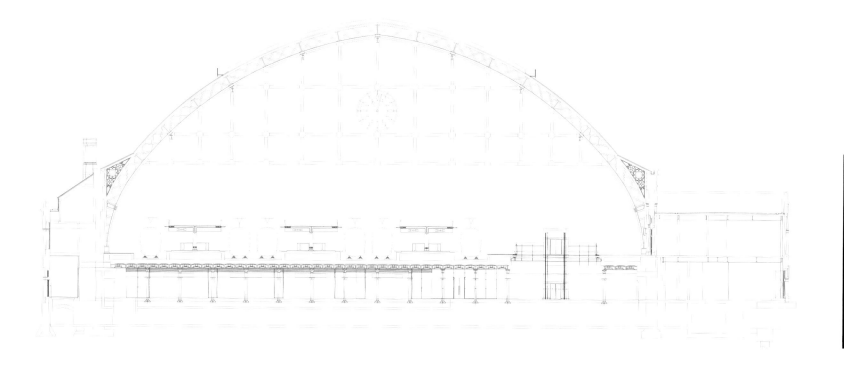

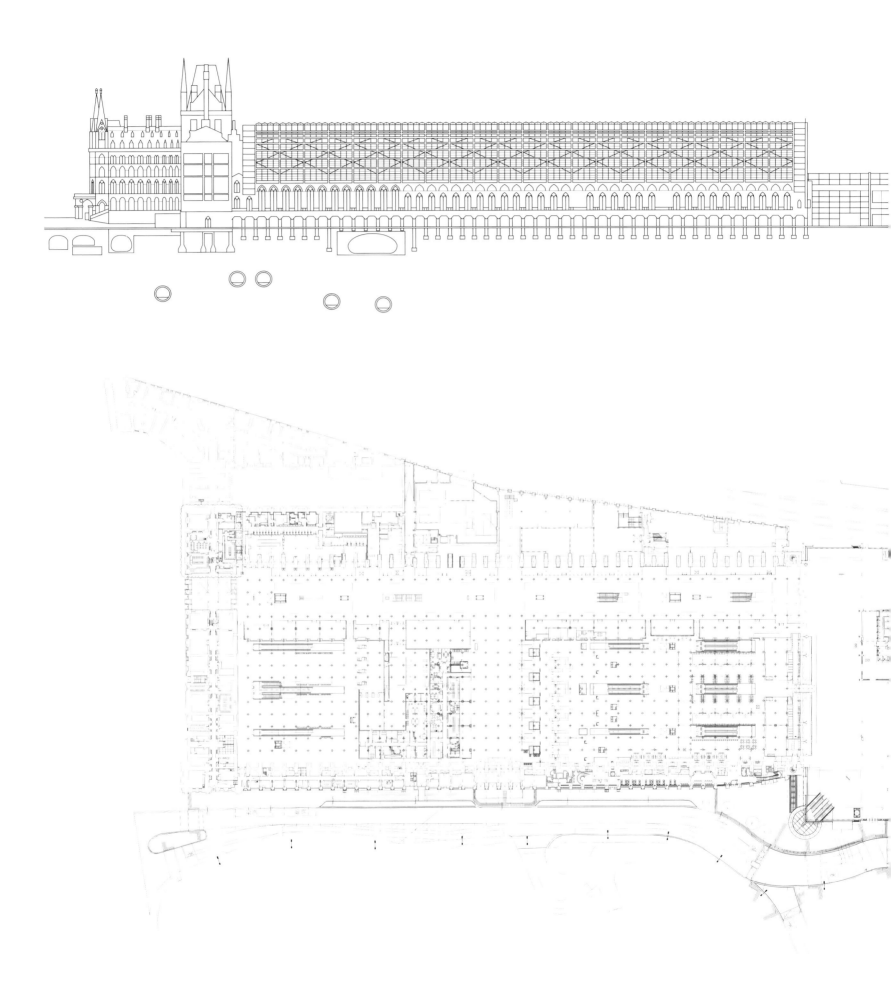

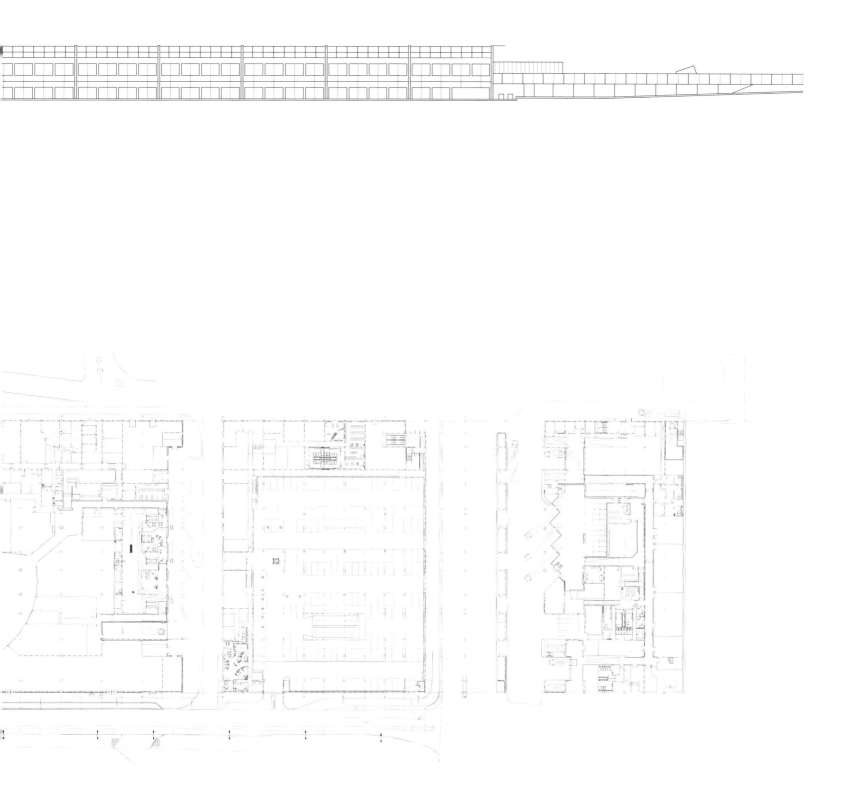

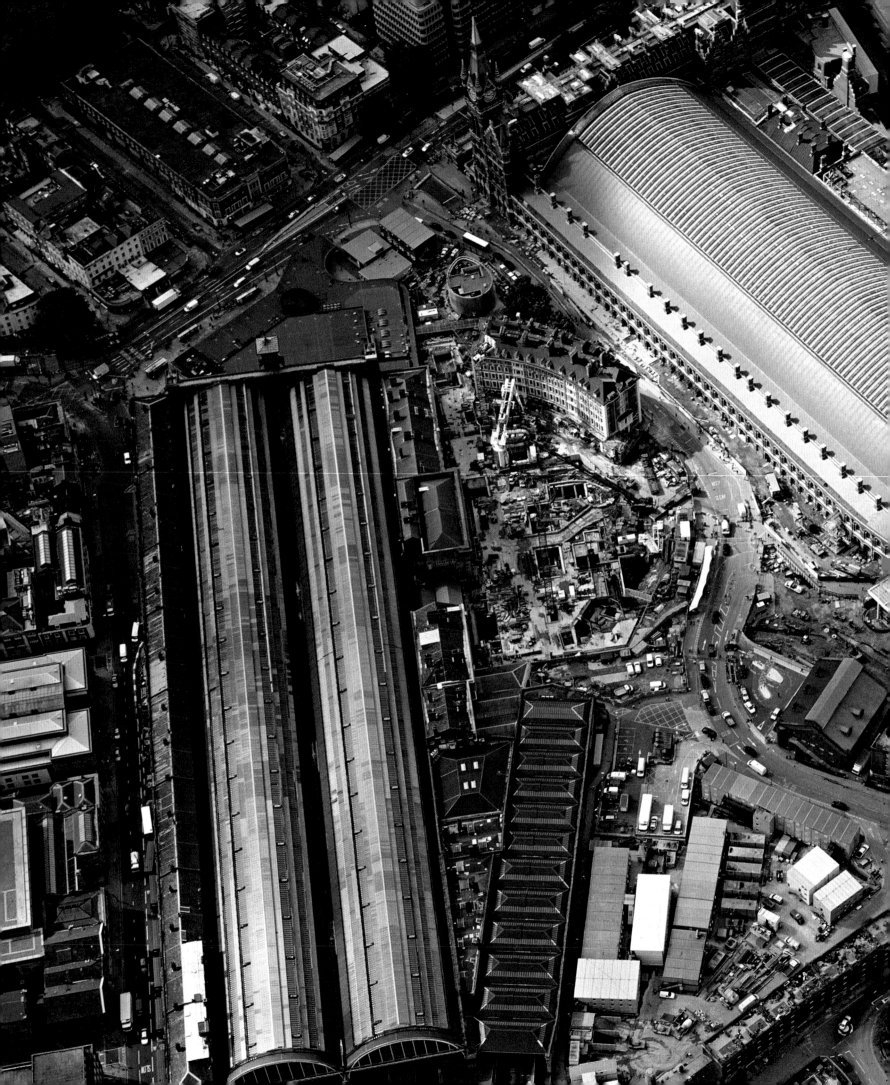

Pages 166–67 St Pancras International from the air, 2007.

Pages 168–69 The magnificent train shed, looking north.

Opposite and this page W.H. Barlow's Victorian ironwork has been meticulously restored.

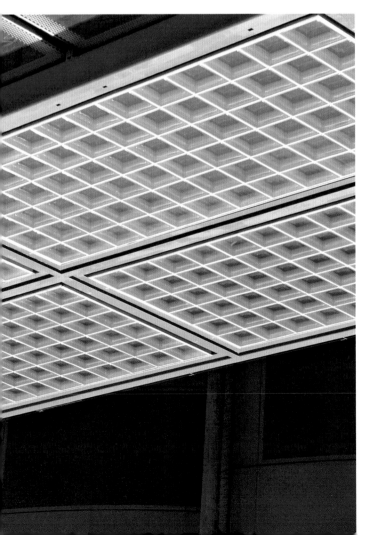

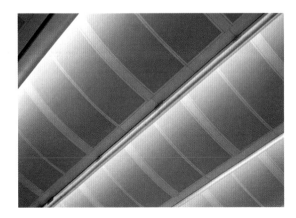

The new train shed
at St Pancras uses
a spare and elegant
architectural language
that is unambiguously
contemporary: an
exhilarating contrast to
W.H. Barlow's exuberant
Victorian engineering.

SCULPTURES

Unusually for a railway station, St Pancras International has an arts policy, and public sculpture has been a controversial feature of the restoration. Strange that although the architectural historian Nikolaus Pevsner was at least as important as the poet John Betjeman in saving the Victorian station, Betjeman got the memorial, not the founder of the Victorian Society. The Poet Laureate's statue is by Martin Jennings, a slightly larger-than-life piece between the champagne bar and the platforms. Betjeman is shown holding Archie, his stuffed bear, in a string bag as he admires W.H. Barlow's roof. 'Welcome to the cathedral of all our hellos and goodbyes', he may be thinking.

Paul Day attracted some notice with a Battle of Britain memorial on London's Victoria Embankment. LCR audaciously commissioned a monumental sculpture, intended to evoke the romance of travel. The result was *The Meeting Place*, a gigantic couple sharing an embrace, appropriately suggestive for a station of coming and going.

'Art is not only there to be looked at but also to help people learn to look beyond the artwork to the environment surrounding it and them. The Meeting Place expresses the romance so often attached to train travel. On entering the station, the traveller passes through a gateway into a grand, visionary architecture, a world of travel that links London to Paris, Brussels and the great Beyond.'
                    Paul Day, *The Meeting Place*

Opposite A computer-generated image of the Midland Grand Hotel after restoration.

Above The restaurant (top) and bar of the new hotel.

Right The western elevation of St Pancras International, showing the new hotel extension.

twenty-first-century train shed has been added to the Victorian original. Since a Eurostar of eighteen cars is about 400 metres long, a 240-metre extension of the original platforms was required. This extension is a rectilinear steel frame supported on 20-metre-tall columns, the whole clad in aluminium louvres and glass. It accommodates six Eurostar platforms, three domestic high-speed lines and four platforms for the Midland Mainline tracks. To some eyes it mates heroically and confidently with Barlow's design, to others the effect is more discordant. Indisputably, the whole adds a third massive element to a structure with an already grandiose sequence of spaces. It is quite literally breathtaking.

A new hotel and apartments, developed by the Manhattan Loft Corporation with Renaissance Marriott as the hotel operator, will open in 2010 in Scott's building and a cleverly inserted addition facing the British Library. The original glass-box design for the new block, by Renton Howard Wood Levin, was rejected by English Heritage (the government's advisor on the historic environment), which called for something, if not 'feeble and forged', then certainly in 'the Scott manner'. The new building was duly delivered by conservation architects Richard Griffiths Architects. This firm had worked, to general approval, on the millennium buildings at Southwark Cathedral, on the south bank of the River Thames, where an eclectic architectural mix in a sacred and historic setting was handled with great tact. William Morris, founder of the Society for the Protection of Ancient Buildings, had a useful term for that major problem facing conservation architects. He called it 'honest repair'. The issue is to avoid brainless pastiche, while making improvements in sympathy with the existing structure. More or less in pursuit of the 'Scott manner' on which English Heritage had insisted, Griffiths settled for Gothic pointed arches. Although he had considered square-topped windows as an alternative, he accepted that Scott's original composition of the hotel façade was ingenious. He did not copy it, but rather used it as a starting point, producing a new design with interesting sophistications. To cope with a lot of anticipated turbulent activity below – Barlow himself called it 'racking motion' – prudent movement joints were called for in the brickwork, but they are carefully concealed; two floors are, in addition, artfully disguised as a coherent single-storey order.

With a reputation for intelligent balance in the sometimes hysterical battle of the architectural styles, Griffiths explains that the style he created in his

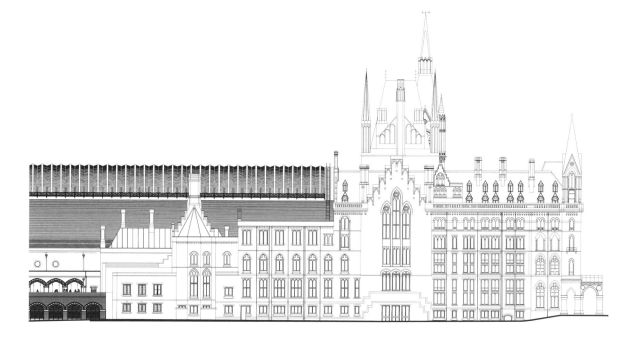

When it opened in the mid-nineteenth century St Pancras was one of the greatest stations in the country. But in its darkest days, when it let St Pancras fall into slovenly desuetude, British Rail sold the station's famous clock to an American collector. This plan was compromised when workers removing the timepiece dropped it.

The wreckage of the original, made by Dent – who also manufactured Parliament's famous clock – was salvaged by Roland Hoggard and painstakingly restored in his Nottingham garden over a period of eighteen months. His fastidious remedial work allowed an exact copy to be made for St Pancras International.

Below The Champagne
Bar at St Pancras
International has been
successfully promoted as
'the longest in the world'.

Opposite St Pancras
International is intended
to be a destination in its
own right.

red-brick new-build was 'a more constructive Gothic – more Philip Webb than Scott, perhaps, omitting some of the richness of decoration and bringing out what lies behind that'.

Bringing HS1 to life

With building work essentially finished, what remained before the inaugural service on 14 November 2007 was to 'bring the railway to life': powering up lines, checking calibrations, and familiarizing staff and travellers. The London-to-Paris journey time has been reduced to 135 minutes, but £5.8 billion was not spent to save a few minutes for twenty-first-century *flâneurs*. The new St Pancras is about urban regeneration and a national commitment to rail travel: from 2009 high-speed domestic lines using St Pancras will change the perception of rail travel within the British Isles, just as the TGV did in France.

But best of all is the achievement of turning St Pancras from a grim conservationist's lost cause into an attractive destination in its own right. It is possibly now the finest station in the world, a winning mixture of great tradition, high technology and impeccable style. It contains Europe's longest champagne bar (at 92 metres), plus proper restaurants and serious shops.

LCR researched what people actually do in stations. Behavioural psychologists have discovered that, because of anxieties and perceived pressures, the field of consciousness in airports is reduced to a defensive radius of about 1.5 metres, so that the impact of the architecture scarcely registers. Stations are different. Research shows that international rail travellers have a 'dwell time' of thirty-seven minutes, of which seven are reserved for shopping.

St Pancras has a welcome service, made possible by a four-fold increase in staff on the ground. Mike Luddy, project director for LCRSP (LCR's stations and property division), in charge of retail and other station services, was determined to change the way stations are conceived in terms of customer service. Traditionally, both airports and stations kept operations and commercial outlets separate, with occasionally ruinous results, as at Stansted Airport, north of London, where the architect Norman Foster's bold concept of transparency and clarity was immediately compromised by an interest in selling socks and smoked salmon.

The benchmark for St Pancras International was New York's magnificent Grand Central station: a mixture of railway terminus, shops, bars, restaurants and romance.

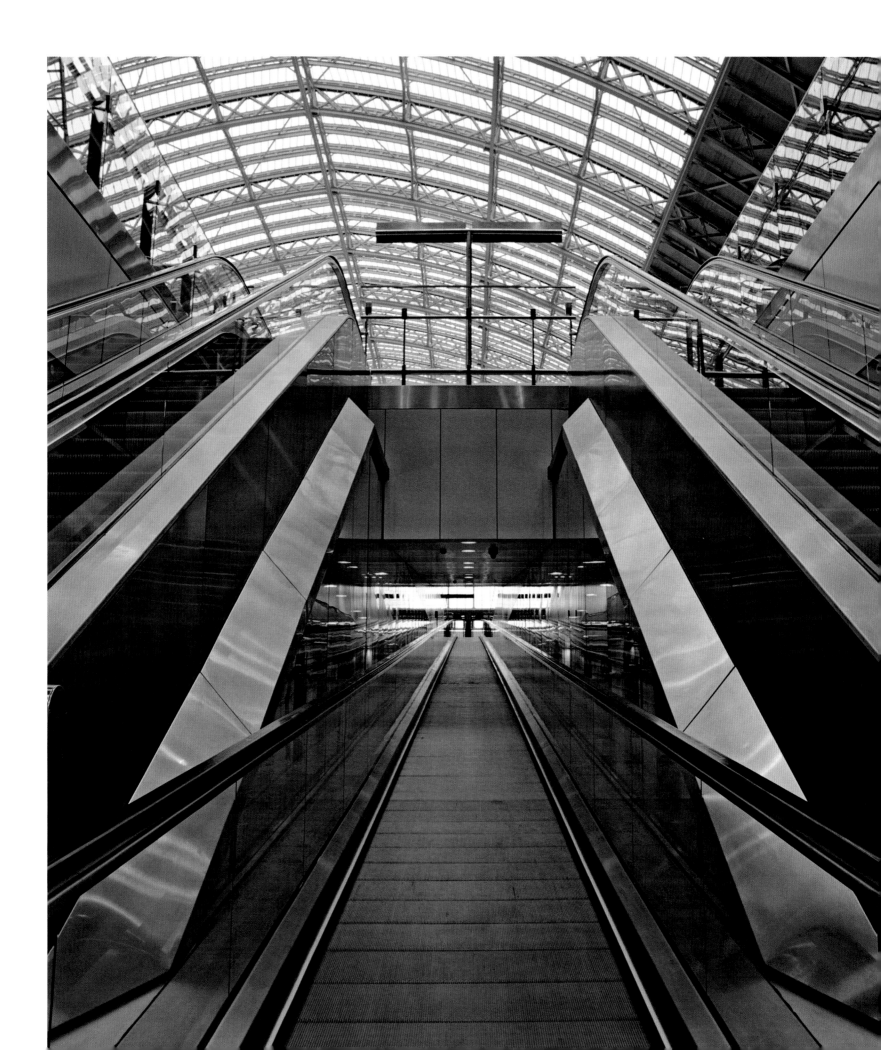

LE TRAIN BLEU

Le Train Bleu in the Gare de Lyon, Paris, is, with Grand Central's Oyster Bar, the *beau idéal* of all station restaurants. Located on a mezzanine above the concourse, it is a mind-bogglingly opulent exercise in decoration, with its crystal chandeliers, floral offerings, sconces, stucco and statues. The station was built for the Exposition Universelle of 1900, and the restaurant opened the following year. Eleven-metre-high paintings of delights and destinations in southern France are shown here: Nice, Monte Carlo, Antibes, Orange and Marseilles, all evoking the 'mythique ligne PLM'. Diners sit on wood-framed brown-leather banquettes with brass fittings, enjoying 'recettes classiques et plats de brasserie'.

Le Train Bleu at the Gare de Lyon, Paris: an Art Nouveau masterpiece of 1900.

The benchmark was New York's Grand Central station, which, like St Pancras, was once run-down. Grand Central has exceptionally high standards of cleanliness. Like the manufacturer and philanthropist Lord Lever, who believed that happy workers are good workers, the operators of HS1 consider that a benign environment makes customers happy and more disposed to the culture of shopping. But the primary task, Luddy suggests, is to soothe them with good information systems and a pleasant, unthreatening environment, so that buying socks seems not so much an end in itself, but rather an entirely natural thing to do. The marvellous French expression *folie de gare* describes the anxieties and panic of the old world of travel where the passenger was construed as a brainless victim rather than a privileged customer. At St Pancras everything is being done to make *folie de gare* a thing of the past. There are eleven pods with live information and real-time screens in each of sixty-three shops, so while buying coffee you are still informed about the lively possibility of missing your train. And the character of the shops is different. At Waterloo International it was found that when a dated and weary shirt shop was changed to a premium one, turnover went up 70 per cent. Shopping at St Pancras is influenced by that observation.

When they have orientated themselves with intelligent signage and found that they have more time to spend, HS1 travellers find St Pancras full of diversions. The station expects to become a destination – literally, *vaut le voyage* – for the seven to ten million visitors who do not actually want to go to the West End to shop. With upmarket food and clothing outlets and a farmers' market, it is a new model for railway service.

GRAND CENTRAL, NEW YORK:
THE DESTINATION STATION

New York's Grand Central is the ultimate destination railway station. As the model for the new St Pancras, it is returning a compliment: the original station of 1871 used the same openwork iron arches tied by beams beneath the platforms as W.H. Barlow had used at St Pancras. It is, by some measures, the largest railway station in the world, with forty-four platforms. Certainly, the majestic concourse boasts of American imperial splendour. Actually, it is a terminus, not a station, since it is the end of the line. But that enhances the drama. The American radio show of 1937, *Grand Central Station*, famously summed up the terminus in its opening words: 'As a bullet seeks its target, shining rails in every part of our great country are aimed at Grand Central Station ... . Day and night, great trains rush toward the Hudson River ... dive with a roar into the two and one-half mile tunnel that burrows beneath the swank and glitter of Park Avenue. And then ... Grand Central Station! – crossroads of a million private lives, gigantic stage on which are played a thousand dramas daily.'

As in the case of HS1, many architects, engineers and designers were involved in the creation of Grand Central. The railroad's chief engineer, William Wilgus, called for a new terminus on Park Avenue. The firm of Reed & Stem won a limited competition for the design in 1913, the important elements of which included the separation of trains, subway, cars and people. Later, Whitney Warren of Warren & Wetmore, a swish

New York practice, added Beaux Arts grandeur to the practical arrangements. Between 1994 and 1998 Grand Central was subject to a thorough-going refurbishment: the Tennessee quarry that had provided the original stone was reopened for the purpose. And the famous Oyster Bar, which, along with Le Train Bleu, is one of the best railway restaurants in the world, was also brought up to date. This is no apologetic franchise offering timid industrialized

catering, but the sort of place where rushing New Yorkers can eat a dozen Belons or Chincoteagues on the half-shell while standing, as they did in the nineteenth century. Or, with time to spare, enjoy a fillet of tautog with boiled potatoes and fiddlehead ferns in the more formal restaurant or clubby tavern.

Below Her Majesty The
Queen opens St Pancras
International station,
6 November 2007.

Opposite The station seen
from Pancras Road on
the night of the opening
ceremony.

6 November 2007

On a clear and very cold November night a curious and overcoated crowd queued patiently to take its seats at the Royal opening of the new St Pancras International station. There were all the attendant goings-on familiar in our paranoid times: hi-vis security men importantly following silent commands in their ear-buds, screens, fences, blue flashing lights, frisks, photo ID. Waiting. And then more waiting under that wall of red brick. If you cared about these things, you could muse that the great historian of Georgian London, the somewhat epicene Sir John Summerson, found this swaggering Victorian assemblage of retrieved tectonic memory 'nauseating'. Most people were just freezing.

But the crowd was evidence that now St Pancras has become a lot of other things, too. Teaser advertising campaigns had excited real curiosity. Newspapers had published aerial photographs showing the true, vast extent of works that most of the population had been ignorant of or indifferent to. From the air, the picture is entirely different. These long, desolate 'railway lands' of King's Cross, once devoted to imperial trade but more recently turned over to rough trade, crack-whores and the wrong sort of kebabs, have been turned into a diagram of the future.

The ornate face is still there and Barlow's shed has been made new, but the fresh reality at the heart of St Pancras is: London now has the world's most impressive railway station, one that is intended to become a destination in its own right. A station once in a shamefully neglected state is now a temple where the new rites of high-speed terrestrial travel are observed. This is what we were waiting to see.

Station opening ceremonies are very rare: they had one at Berlin's new Hauptbahnhof in 2006 and in Liverpool in 1830 (when, on the ceremonial return journey to Manchester, the Liverpool MP William Huskisson was most unfortunately run over as the locomotive took on water at Newton-le-Willows, becoming the first railway fatality). So it was an extraordinary experience to attend one, even to queue for one. Some restive members of the crocodile were mumbling about the Millennium Dome crowd-control calamity. Someone said that with so many greybeards around it was like a Rolling Stones concert.

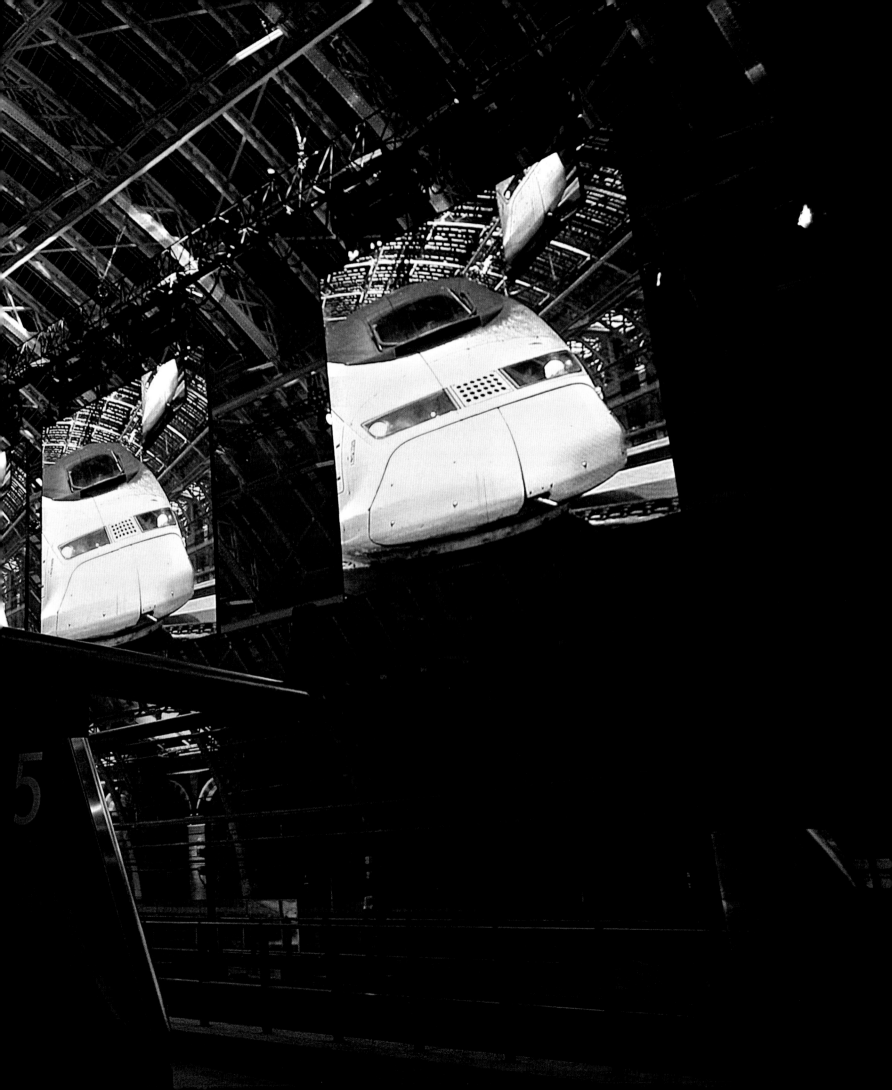

Vignettes from the opening,
6 November 2007: the
restored Dent clock (right);
the Royal Philharmonic
Concert Orchestra
(opposite); and a
spectacular of modern
event management
(previous pages and below).

But this was altogether more intelligent than the Dome and more ambitious than the Stones. The crowd was queueing to see not just a station, but the source of entirely new infrastructure that will redraw our geographical and mental maps. The ceremony was a bit of a phantasmagoria, like the station: a spectacular of modern event-management with choreographed giant screens, light shows and a frenetic Royal Philharmonic Concert Orchestra. Timothy West put on a stovepipe hat to play W.H. Barlow. Certainly, Her Majesty perhaps mused, railways have changed since Queen Victoria's and Barlow's, let alone Betjeman's, day.

St Pancras is wonderful. Maybe the sentimental will wonder what Scott and Barlow would have made of French and Japanese electric trains whooshing nearly silently into platforms (Eurocratically also denominated as 'Quais') where mighty 4-6-2s once puffed. It is strange to recall that British engineers were influential during the early years of the French railways: William Buddicom built locomotives for the Paris–Le Havre line at his factory in Rouen; an engine designed by Thomas Crampton was the last train out of Paris when it was under siege by the Prussians in 1870; and Alfred de Glehn, English despite his name, became engineering director of the Société Alsacienne de Constructions Mecaniques. Glehn's technique of 'compounding' (involving extending the cycle of the high-pressure steam by using it in more than one cylinder) remained the French standard until well into the twentieth century.

Below, left One of the first
Eurostar passengers at
St Pancras International.

Below, right A Eurostar
prepares to leave
St Pancras International
to realize a dream of
seamless European travel.

**Opposite and pages
198–99** High-speed
escalators serve the
high-speed trains.

14 November 2007

On 14 November 2007 the first Eurostar left St Pancras at 11.03. Here was the conclusion of a dream about seamless European travel that had begun when Europhobia in 1751 led to the very first proposals for a Channel Tunnel. The British were still resisting it in the 1920s when the superlatively xenophobic Earl of Crawford and Balcarres warned of the dangers of a tunnel to Europe.

This conclusion was witnessed from an ambitiously long champagne bar by hundreds of passengers keen to appreciate the hedonistic reality of the new age of the train. The technology and the champagne might be French, but the desire is British. HS1 has been built to the largest of the International Union of Railways gauges, which means (at least in theory) that French TGVs and German ICEs can freely penetrate the Garden of England. The sheer romance is back.

Regeneration

This section is being written within the space of a twenty-first-century high-speed journey from London to Paris. I am thinking of my favourite Parisian bistro, but that will have to wait; as the 300-kilometre-per-hour Eurostar pulls ever so slowly away from the platform, one falls to wondering what all this means for London and the south-east of England. Forget Paris and its alluring pleasures for a moment; it is not just a matter of getting the *flâneur* to Paris more quickly. From 2009 new domestic high-speed services using the same track will liberate east Kent, taking commuters hither and yon at 225 kilometres per hour.

Below Ebbsfleet in the future. The new transport link is the first part of a planned transformation of this desolate part of the Thames Gateway.

Bottom Stratford's Southern Land Bridge is one of four land bridges linking the different parts of the Olympic site across railway lines and waterways.

Faversham will become Hammersmith, Sittingbourne will achieve connectivity with the cosmopolis. While Alstom TGVs travel to Europe and back, in 2012 Hitachi Class 395 'Javelins' will get you to the Olympics in Stratford in seven minutes.

The HS1 track is also the main artery of the Thames Gateway, Europe's largest regeneration scheme. The Olympics is the focus, but there is more. The Thames Gateway is a catch-all term for the vast area of industrial dereliction, riverside and bird-centric wetlands that stretches 65 kilometres east from Canary Wharf to Sittingbourne in Kent and Southend in Essex. Frankly depressing (except, perhaps, for the birds), it is already home to 1.45 million people. But the vision is huge. Before HS1, sclerotic transport links frustrated economic development; soon, however, there will be a new port in addition to the new railway. The Olympics is intended to be an accelerator for even larger developments, and by 2016 there will be 160,000 new homes where there are presently only toxic brownfields and their resident curlews.

What will HS1 contribute? Taken together, the three most significant regenerated sites belonging to the new railway – St Pancras itself, plus Stratford and Ebbsfleet stations – will create more jobs than Canary Wharf, more homes than anywhere else in the south-east and more shops than the Bluewater or Lakeside shopping centres. At Stratford, spoil from the London Tunnel spewed out by the thunderous TBMs has been efficiently used to raise the level of the site of the new Stratford City by 7 metres, helpfully above the Thames's troublesome flood plain. At 50 hectares, Stratford City is about the size of London's Green Park. It means 34,000 new jobs, 5500 homes, 2000 hotel rooms and 140,000 square metres of retail. Ebbsfleet, the second station on the new track, will be a country town the size of Chichester by 2027.

Life will be harder for the crack-whores, minicabs and kebab merchants who once made the area their own, but one of the new things people are going to say about St Pancras is 'meet me there'. And it is not the only station that will benefit. A terminus that is being lauded as a true destination station will be the catalyst for King's Cross Central, an ambitious and responsible 780,000-square-metre mixed-use development around King's Cross, now known as KX2.0, which will provide two thousand new homes, fifty new buildings, twenty new public streets and ten major new public spaces. More than 40 per cent of this revived and rejuvenated brownfield site, formerly railway lands, will be public realm, with three new parks, five squares, three new bridges over Regent's Canal and twenty refurbished historic buildings. Wind turbine generators will supply power, while listed gasholder frames will be restored as mementoes of earlier and dirtier energy sources. St Pancras International will not only be remembered as a transformation of epic proportions, a moment when a new breed of engineers and architects dared to make Barlow's great train shed beautiful again. It will also become the jewel in the crown of a vibrant new part of London. For so long a hinterland of monotonous depravity, King's Cross will rise again as an exciting new quarter stitched into the very fabric of London.

Conclusion

Eurostar services began back in 1994 between London and Paris and, lest we forget the unfairly neglected Lillois and Belgians in their flatlands of red brick and beer, Lille and Brussels, too. An initial sense of wonder has given way to a slightly *mondaine* familiarity. People have begun to mutter that some of the romance of travel has disappeared. But, for 'romance', read 'misery'. Because suddenly that least cosmopolitan of places, Ashford, was denominated 'International',

the boulevards of the French capital seemed a little closer to Kent (and therefore rather less chic) than before. Because of this, some people find the visit to Paris a little less exciting than in the past. But what they really mean is that they do not have to endure a lumpy ferry crossing, a harrowing drive down the autoroute or the infernal and murderous circulation on the *Périphérique*. Nor, if avoiding travelling by air, do they have to suffer the humiliations and indignities or delays of Heathrow Airport and, later, the brute infelicities of a *taxi Parisien*.

As Lord Alfred Tennyson, that great beneficiary of the first railway age, said, 'Let the great world spin forever down the ringing grooves of change.' (Later it was revealed that the great poet had misunderstood the fundamental technology and had misconstrued the masculine rails to be feminine grooves. But it had been dark.) Or, as Marcel Proust described his favourite train: 'It seemed to me to cut, at a precise point in every afternoon, a delectable groove, a mysterious mark, from which the diverted hours still led, of course, towards evening, towards tomorrow morning.' The sight of Eurostars, in their own delectable grooves, coming and going from the great Barlow shed, carries a promise of which Tennyson and Proust could only dream. In a flash from St Pancras you swoop underground into that engineered netherworld. You are air-conditioned and comfortable. You are on your way abroad. And, since you will be travelling at high speed, you will get there long before Proust's continuously fugitive 'tomorrow morning'.

Transit Street (top) and Granary Square at the future King's Cross Central development. This stretch of Regent's Canal, once neglected and forsaken, will be the focus of a new city quarter.

Afterword: The end of the line?

Although it is less than three months since the opening of High Speed 1, all of us involved with its delivery and completion have been delighted by the strong public interest, the media acclaim and the boost to Eurostar ticket sales. Britain is now fully connected to the European high-speed rail network; we have a real jewel in the crown, with the restored and iconic St Pancras International station; and we have the transport infrastructure that will support the regeneration of the King's Cross lands, Stratford and the Thames Gateway.

But I believe this country now has something else: hugely restored credibility.

HS1 has demonstrated that the UK actually can deliver complex infrastructure projects, on time and on budget. The project has turned around people's expectations and confidence in the British construction industry.

The government has acknowledged the benefits of supporting the private sector in delivering large complex projects that provide huge social gains as well as meeting private needs.

HS1 was a remarkable engineering achievement, as recognized by Her Majesty The Queen at the Royal Opening of St Pancras International on 6 November 2007. But it has also been defined by true innovation in its attention to a wide range of concerns: archaeology, the environment, community relations, risk sharing, partnering and above all construction safety.

So why has HS1 succeeded where other large infrastructure projects have failed: in meeting the exacting requirements of delivering to time and to budget? I know that describing the commercial framework and project management in the story of HS1 may not seem as enthralling as its bold engineering achievements, but the way this project has been delivered could and should be held up as a model for delivering rail projects in this country in the future. To begin with, the creation of an informed 'client team' in Union Railways provided the continuity that long-term projects demand; the creation of Rail Link Engineering (RLE) as designer and project manager brought together a consortium of real experts in their respective fields (Arup, Bechtel, Halcrow and Systra); and LCR itself provided the connection between those delivering the railway and those who would use it. At the heart of all this has been the concept of 'partnering', an approach that created a powerful blend of unique strengths and generated a strong will to succeed and to overcome the obstacles along the way. Such crucial elements as the Cost Overrun Protection Programme, pioneered by Bechtel, and our model of target-price contracting were at the time unique in the UK construction industry. At all times our ethos was to pass risk to those in the best place to manage it.

Many now ask whether the construction cost of £5.8 billion was worth it. Although many will dispute its value, HS1 is much more than a railway that improves the travelling times and reliability of rail journeys to the Continent and for Kent commuters. HS1 is also about regeneration in some of the most deprived areas of the UK. The provision of this new piece of transport infrastructure is a catalyst for more than £10 billion of further investment, which will bring new jobs, new homes and new communities to regions that have been blighted for generations.

As fascinating and challenging as the last decade has been, it is now much more important to look forward. With HS1, we have connected this country to a high-speed network that, by 2010, will have expanded to 6000 kilometres throughout Europe. And so we in the UK should be looking forward to High Speed 2. With the train increasingly seen as the 'greener' way to travel, there is now, more than ever, a compelling argument to continue the journey.

All those involved in the HS1 project are immensely proud of what has been achieved and delivered. We are also proud of how we have addressed other people's concerns and overcome the obstacles thrown up along the way. However, the most lasting memory will be of the people involved in this amazing project, for what they have achieved individually and as a team.

Rob Holden
CEO, London & Continental Railways
Deputy Chairman, Eurostar
February 2008

CHRONOLOGY

8000 BC The British land mass is still connected to the European mainland.

***c.* 6000 BC** The Anglo-German plain floods, and the English Channel is formed.

1751 The Treaty of Amiens suggests the possibility of a Channel Tunnel.

1799 The first (failed) attempted underwater tunnel between Gravesend, Kent, and Tilbury, Essex.

1818 Marc Isambard Brunel patents a 'tunnel shield'.

1843 (25 March) Brunel's Thames Tunnel in east London opens to pedestrians.

1850 The first submarine telegraphic cable connects Britain physically to Europe.

1862 (24 May) The first London Underground journey by Metropolitan Railway.

1865 (3 May) W.H. Barlow's design for the Midland Railway train shed is approved.

1866 George Gilbert Scott wins the Midland Railway competition to design St Pancras's Midland Grand Hotel.

1872 The English Channel Tunnel Company is formed.

1883 Sir John Hawkshaw reports to Parliament on his geological investigation of the Channel seabed.

1906 Formation of a new Channel Tunnel Company, a joint venture with l'Association du Chemin de Fer Sous-Marin entre la France et l'Angleterre.

1930 The Peacock Committee reports on the desirability of a Channel Tunnel.

1956 The first meetings of the Channel Tunnel Study Group are held.

1963 A Government White Paper finally gives official support for a Channel Tunnel.

1967 St Pancras station becomes a Grade I-listed building.

1971 (June–November) The British Railways Board (BRB) sets up a strategy group to work on Channel Tunnel planning. It emerges that SNCF is planning a network of high-speed lines. SNCF suggests that British Rail (BR) should be working on a similarly designed route between the Channel Tunnel and the outskirts of London. Consultants Livesey & Henderson are engaged to investigate the prospects for a UK high-speed line connecting London Victoria or Kensington Olympia with a station at Saltwood, Kent.

1973 (September) The Channel Tunnel White Paper is published, proposing the Channel Tunnel at a cost of £468 million and a high-speed link to White City in west London at a cost of £120 million.

(15 November) Anglo-French agreement to begin the boring of the Channel Tunnel.

1974 (5 February) BR publishes a proposal for a high-speed line via Saltwood, Smeeth, Ashford, Tonbridge, Crowhurst, South Croydon and Clapham Junction. Models of the proposal are exhibited, and the first indications of environmental protest emerge in Croydon and elsewhere along the route.

(26 November) It is announced to the House of Commons that the timetable for decision-making is not realistic because cheaper options need to be examined. BRB has already identified eight different schemes at different levels of cost and rates of return.

1975 (21 January) The Transport Select Committee reports on the Channel Tunnel Scheme, recommending the use of a larger-diameter tunnel capable of carrying shuttle trains, to cost £806 million.

(25 January) The British government formally withdraws from the Channel Tunnel project and orders a twelve-month moratorium to allow it to investigate cheaper options.

1976 (16 January) The project is formally abandoned. Shareholders are repaid their investment with a premium. The French commitment to build a high-speed link is forgotten by the British government.

1978 (September) BR and SNCF propose a revised Channel Tunnel scheme (subsequently nicknamed 'The Mousehole'), a single tunnel capable of taking traditional passenger and freight trains. In *Cross Channel Rail Link*, published by BR, the cost is given at £650 million, and it is proposed to use existing lines to London.

1979 (February) A scheme for the 'Mousehole' is presented to the British government, with a proposed cost of £752 million. The plan does not include a shuttle terminal or a high-speed link. BR is instructed to absorb the extra trains into its existing network.

1980 (19 March) The Ministry of Transport invites tenders for the construction of the tunnel.

(31 October) The 'Night Ferry' train service between London Victoria, Paris and Brussels is discontinued.

1981 France's *train à grande vitesse* (TGV) begins high-speed rail travel in Europe.

(February) The Transport Select Committee publishes its report on the Channel Tunnel Rail Link (CTRL).

(10–11 September) At a meeting in London President Mitterrand and Prime Minister Thatcher express their enthusiasm for the concept of a fixed link between Britain and France, and agree to set up a joint study of the proposed options.

(October) BR and SNCF publish a Joint Report on a twin-bore tunnel (a single tunnel with a side tunnel for maintenance and emergency use), allowing up to 120 trains per day between Britain and France.

1982 (4 May) The British Cabinet is considering the proposal for a twin-bore tunnel when the sinking of HMS *Sheffield* by a French-built Exocet missile is announced. The decision is deferred until the British–French study group has reported, which it does in June, recommending the twin-bore proposal.

1984 (January) President Mitterrand and Prime Minister Thatcher agree to prepare a proposal for a Channel Tunnel.

1986 (20 January) Prime Minister Thatcher and President Mitterrand announce the winners of the Channel Tunnel contract: Channel Tunnel Group–France Manche.

(12 February) The Treaty of Canterbury on the Channel Tunnel is signed by President Mitterrand

and Prime Minister Thatcher in the Chapter House of Canterbury Cathedral.

1987 (23 July) The Channel Tunnel Act is given Royal Assent. London Waterloo is named as the first terminus for international services.

(29 July) The Anglo-French Fixed Link Treaty is signed in Paris by President Mitterrand and Prime Minister Thatcher. BR begins a study of long-term capacity needed for tunnel services, and King's Cross is chosen as a second station.

(November) BRB commissions a study of the possible routes from the Channel Tunnel portal to central London.

1988 (January) Protest and public consultation begin, as four possible routes are announced.

(July) BR's report on the effects of the CTRL is published. The design team's lack of understanding about the impact of a new railway causes widespread anxiety, and protests against the new line are held in Kent and Trafalgar Square, London.

1989 (24 March) The first single route option, an amalgam of those previously studied, is announced publicly to reduce uncertainty.

(September) The CTRL's route is refined as a result of local and county consultation, and public consultation begins.

(18 December) BR and SNCF sign a £500 million contract for the purchase of thirty high-speed trains for the international services between Paris, London and Brussels.

1990 (June) Secretary of State Cecil Parkinson rejects the BRB proposals. The route between the Channel Tunnel and the River Medway is accepted and safeguarded. Parkinson widens the brief to the project team by asking the joint venture to evaluate routes from the Medway to central London in more detail, improve the benefits to domestic and international passengers, develop a freight strategy and evaluate routes proposed by other people.

(1 December) British and French flags are exchanged underwater following Channel Tunnel breakthrough.

1991 (May) Plans for southerly and easterly CTRL routes are submitted to the Department of Transport.

(October) A north-easterly route is finally determined for CTRL, because of the regeneration benefits.

1992 (28 July) A new company, Union Railways, is formed to develop and construct the new line. Its workforce consists of public- and private-sector staff, BR technical experts, eight private-sector engineering consultancies and eight environmental consultancies.

1993 Union Railways is appointed to oversee the CTRL project, and announces initial plans for its construction. Production of Eurostar trains begins.

(22 March) The government's preferred route from the Channel Tunnel as far as Barking, east London, is announced, along with two options between Barking and King's Cross/St Pancras.

(17 May) Waterloo International station is completed. Services cannot begin for a year because the Channel Tunnel is not ready for operation until May 1994.

1994 (24 January) St Pancras is named as the London terminus of an easterly route from the Channel Tunnel.

(February) A competition is launched to appoint a private-sector promoter to design, build, finance and operate the CTRL.

(6 May) Her Majesty The Queen opens the Channel Tunnel to commercial traffic.

(9 June) Nine consortia bid to take charge of the CTRL project, and four are selected to submit full proposals: Green Arrow, Eurorail, London & Continental Railways (LCR) and Union Link.

(August) An intermediate station at Ebbsfleet in north Kent is announced, following the confirmation of the route via Pepper Hill and Ashford.

(14 November) Eurostar inaugural service from London Waterloo to Gare du Nord, Paris.

1995 (June) LCR and Eurorail are shortlisted for the final stage of the competition to control the CTRL.

1996 (29 February) The concession to create and manage the CTRL and Eurostar is given to LCR. With the appointment of LCR comes the decision to include a station at Stratford, a crucial part of the company's commercial strategy.

(December) The Channel Tunnel Rail Link Act 1996 is authorized by Parliament.

1997 (March) Rail Link Engineering (RLE) is the new name for the joint venture that will design and manage the construction of CTRL. RLE consists of Arup, Bechtel, Halcrow and Systra.

1998 (January) There is growing concern that LCR's traffic projections and the revenue predictions based on them are unrealistic, following optimistic passenger forecasts. On 28 January Deputy Prime Minister John Prescott announces to the House of Commons that LCR is unable to raise the finance for the project.

(3 June) The government accepts a revised proposal by LCR: that Railtrack will underwrite the construction of one phase (Section 1, Channel Tunnel–Southfleet) of the CTRL and will acquire it on completion, and has an option to do the same for the second phase (Section 2, Southfleet–St Pancras International).

(15 October) John Prescott attends the groundbreaking ceremony on the west bank of the River Medway as work begins on-site to construct Section 1 of the CTRL.

1999 (February) Union Railways (South) and Union Railways (North) will be the client organizations responsible for sections 1 and 2 respectively.

(7 June) Planting programme of 1.2 million native trees begins. The first phase is for 45,000 trees to replace those lost to the railway earthworks.

(1 September) CTRL announces the extent of the ecological programme associated with the construction of the new railway.

2000 (7 February) The Medway Viaduct begins to take shape as the first deck section is slid out over the piers.

(8 June) John Prescott is guest of honour at the breakthrough of the UK's first high-speed rail tunnel, under the North Downs in Kent.

(7 July) Bridge House at Mersham, Kent, is slid 55 metres to a new location away from the works.

(15 October) The halfway mark for Section 1 is reached. So far, 10 million person-hours have been expended, 13 million cubic metres of earth removed, 8000 foundation piles installed, 300,000 cubic metres of concrete poured, 100,000 trees planted and 11 listed buildings relocated.

2001 (3 April) Railtrack, which is in financial difficulties, relinquishes its option to underwrite Section 2 of CTRL. The government approves LCR's alternative proposals to finance Section 2 with a new plan developed for LCR by Bechtel, its founder shareholder. At St Pancras Chambers in London, an agreement is signed to begin the works on Section 2.

(12 April) The final section of the approach spans of the Medway Viaduct is slid into place.

(2 July) Transport Minister John Spellar MP gives the signal for work to begin on Section 2 of the CTRL with a groundbreaking ceremony at Stratford.

(30 July) The North Downs tunnel is completed early and under budget.

2002 (27 June) Railtrack's ownership of the British rail network is taken over by Network Rail. LCR has agreed terms with Railtrack to buy its interest in Section 1 of the CTRL.

(29 August) Work begins on the London Tunnels. The tunnel-boring machine 'Annie' is expected to bore 95 metres per week towards King's Cross.

(25–27 December) Two CTRL bridges are slid into place behind St Pancras station, over the Midland Mainline tracks, during a Christmas track blockade.

2003 (8 February) Subsidence occurs in a back garden in Stratford, east London, following the passage of a tunnel-boring machine. Thirty-six residents are evacuated as a precaution.

(17 March) Thames Tunnel breakthrough. 'Milly the Muncher Cruncher' reaches the end of the down-line drive from Swanscombe to Thurrock.

(21 March) Alan Titchmarsh plants the millionth tree of the project at Boxley, Kent.

(9 June) End of engineering work on Section 1.

(30 July) Eurostar breaks the UK rail speed record with a speed of 334.7 kilometres per hour on the CTRL, as Section 1 is officially tested.

(28 September) The Prime Minister, Tony Blair, opens Section 1 for commercial services. It becomes Britain's first new inter-urban route in a century.

(14 November) The final span of the Thurrock Viaduct is push-launched into place.

(24–27 December) The CTRL bridge over the East Coast Main Line at King's Cross is slid into position during the Christmas holiday.

2004 (27 January) London Tunnel breakthrough on Section 2.

(23 March) A ceremony at Stratford follows the completion of the London Tunnels by six tunnel-boring machines.

(9–12 April) W.H. Barlow's train shed at St Pancras closes for renovation, and Midland Mainline services transfer temporarily to the eastern side of the extension.

(16 June) The skeleton of *Palaeoloxodon antiquus*, the 400,000-year-old elephant, is found at Ebbsfleet.

(11 September) Cross-London Thameslink services are suspended for six months to allow the new Thameslink station 'box' to be constructed beneath Midland Road.

2005 (17 February) The International Olympic Committee's (IOC) evaluation team for the 2012 Games is driven from Stratford to St Pancras through the CTRL tunnels to demonstrate the plans for the proposed Olympic shuttle.

(12 October) Her Majesty The Queen visits Stratford International station to celebrate London's successful bid for the 2012 Olympics.

2006 (17 July) The western half of the St Pancras extension is completed on time, and Midland Mainline moves to its new home, platforms 1–4.

2007 (7 January) The overhead power lines on Section 2 are electrified at 25,000 volts.

(6 March) The first Eurostar enters St Pancras on a test run.

(12 June) A Eurostar carries the IOC from Stratford to St Pancras in less than seven minutes, demonstrating the potential of the Olympic 'Javelin' domestic shuttle.

(4 September) A Eurostar achieves the fastest rail journey between Paris and London: 2 hours 3 minutes.

(2 October) The Temple Mills depot opens, replacing the North Pole depot in west London as the location for the servicing of Eurostars.

(6 November) The CTRL, now High Speed 1 (HS1), is opened at St Pancras by Her Majesty The Queen.

(14 November) Inaugural service of HS1.

GLOSSARY

AIG American International Group.

COPP Cost-Overrun Protection Plan, a financial arrangement put in place to fund HS1, developed by Bechtel.

CORBER The contractor that completed the restoration of St Pancras, a consortium of Costain, Laing O'Rourke, Bachy Soletanche and Emcor.

CTRL Channel Tunnel Rail Link.

EDF Électricité de France.

Eurostar The high-speed trains (European TGVs) that operate on the route between London, Paris and Brussels, through the Channel Tunnel.

HS1 High Speed 1, the new name of the CTRL (Channel Tunnel Rail Link). HS1 is managed by the designer and project manager RLE.

LCR London & Continental Railways, the builder and operator of HS1 chosen by the government in 1996. LCR is a consortium of Bechtel, Arup, Systra, Halcrow, National Express, SNCF, EDF and UBS. LCR had two operating subsidiaries: Union Railways (South), in charge of Section 1, and Union Railways (North), in charge of Section 2.

LCRSP London & Continental Railways Stations & Property, the team that obtained the land, developed the stations and manages the subsequent property developments.

RLE Rail Link Engineering, a consortium of Arup, Bechtel, Halcrow and Systra, the firms among LCR shareholders providing engineering expertise.

Section 1 The part of HS1 that runs from the Channel Tunnel to the outskirts of London; 74 kilometres long.

Section 2 The urban part of HS1, running from the outskirts of London into St Pancras International station; 38 kilometres long.

SNCB Société Nationale des Chemins de Fer Belges (Belgian national railway).

SNCF Société Nationale des Chemins de Fer (French national railway).

TBM Tunnel-boring machine.

TGV *Train à grande vitesse*, or high-speed train.

UBS Union Bank of Switzerland.

Union Railways The client team that directed RLE.

TECHNICAL

High-speed rail journey times (in minutes) from St Pancras station, central London:
Stratford 7
Ebbsfleet 17
Ashford 26
Channel Tunnel 31
Lille 80
Brussels 111
Paris 135
Barcelona 420 (by 2010)

Eurostar: technical specification
Build: 1993–95
Top speed: 300 kilometres per hour
Power supply: 25kV 50hz AC overhead; 750V DC via the third rail
Traction: Twelve 3-phase asynchronous motors producing 1100kW, equivalent to 16,300hp
Performance metrics: 16kW/ton; 15.9kW/seat
Length: 394 metres (two power cars, eighteen carriages)
Weight: 752 tons

Hitachi Class 395: technical specification
Build: 2004–2007
Top speed: 225 kilometres per hour
Power supply: 25kV 50hz AC overhead; 750V DC via the third rail
Traction: Four IGBT traction packages; sixteen 3-phase asynchronous motors producing 210kW, equivalent to 4506hp
Performance metrics: 12.4kW/ton; 9.3kW/seat
Length: 121.8 metres (two driving powercars, four standard carriages)
Weight: 270 tons

Who supplies the track?
Rails: Corus UK
Sleepers: Stanton Bonna
Fastenings: Vossloh
Pads: Getzner and Sogo
Ballast: Stema
Switches: Vossloh Cogifer
Electrification equipment: Arcelor, TLM, Galland, Gilibert, Nexans, Fullmen, Alstom

London Tunnel facts
The big London Tunnel on Section 2 has five 7.15-metre-bore ventilation shafts, the deepest of which is 60 metres. There are transverse safety cross-passages approximately every 600 metres. Ventilation is an absolute priority, both in terms of supplying fresh air and also in managing the airflow in the tunnels (especially in the event of what is so decorously known as an 'incident', as smoke kills).

Channel Tunnel facts
There are two running tunnels, each measuring 7.7 metres in inner diameter, and a service tunnel of 5 metres inner diameter.

Bored through cretaceous chalk marl, they are an average of 50 metres below the seabed and approximately 30 metres apart.

The tunnels are lined with concrete rings, each 1.5 metres long, sealed with extremely high-specification grout.

The total length is 51 kilometres, of which 37.5 kilometres are underwater.

Chilled water is piped through conduits to keep the tunnels cool.

INDEX

First published 2008 by Merrell Publishers Limited

Head office:
81 Southwark Street
London SE1 0HX

New York office:
740 Broadway, Suite 1202
New York, NY 10003

merrellpublishers.com

British Library Cataloguing-in-Publication Data:
Bayley, Stephen
Work: the building of the Channel Tunnel Rail Link
1. Railroad engineering – England – Kent 2. Railroad engineering
– England – London 3. Railroads – England – Kent – Design
and construction 4. Railroads – England – London – Design and
construction 5. Channel Tunnel (England and France)
I. Title
625.1'0094223

Trade edition
ISBN-13: 978-1-8589-4398-5
ISBN-10: 1-8589-4398-1
Special edition
ISBN-13: 978-1-8589-4464-7
ISBN-10: 1-8589-4464-3

Produced by Merrell Publishers Limited
Designed by IC2
Picture-researched by Sophie Spencer-Wood and Sarah Smithies
Additional text and chronology by Peter Davies and Alan Dyke
Copy-edited by Sarah Yates and Rosanna Fairhead
Proof-read by Nicola Homer
Indexed by Hilary Bird
Printed and bound in Italy